# LIKE A BULGING WALL

*WILL YOU SURVIVE THE 1990's ECONOMIC CRASH?*

## ROBERT BORRUD

# LIKE A BULGING WALL

## WILL YOU SURVIVE THE 1990's ECONOMIC CRASH?

## ROBERT BORRUD

STARBURST PUBLISHERS

P.O. Box 4123, Lancaster, Pennsylvania 17604

To schedule Author appearances write:
Author Appearances, Starburst Promotions, P.O. Box 4123,
Lancaster, PA 17604 or call (717)-293-0939.

## Credits:

Unless otherwise noted, all Scripture quotations are from the New American
Standard Version

Cover Art by Kerne Erickson.

**LIKE A BULGING WALL—Will You Survive
The 1990's Economic Crash?**

First Printing, April 1991

ISBN: 0-914984-28-4
Library of Congress Catalog Number 91-65104

Printed in the United States of America

# Dedication

To my loving wife, *Joyce,*
and
to *Pastor George Voeks,*
who taught us to set our affections
on the Lord Jesus Christ.

# Acknowledgments

*Reverend Richard Borrud,*
for helping me review the manuscript.

*Pastor Bill Pratt,*
*Jerry and Arlene Hagstrom,* and *Syd Stephen,*
for their support and prayers.

My wife, *Joyce,*
for her help with the
graphs and manuscript correction.

# Contents

# Preface

In 1985 David Wilkerson wrote the book *Set The Trumpet To Thy Mouth* in which he had a vision of future judgement upon America. In this vision he saw two lesser calamities which would precede this final judgement.

In the first calamity he saw bombs falling in the Middle East and the smoke of burning oil fields rising day and night. With the culmination of the Middle East war and over 500 Kuwaiti oil wells on fire, this seems to be a startling fulfillment of the first calamity.

In the second calamity he saw a coming economic collapse. *Like A Bulging Wall* focuses on the potential of such a collapse. In this book I discuss the seeds of this possible calamity, its causes, and its effects on our lives. Even now, we are beginning to experience the troubles of this approaching "crash."

It is my prayer that this book will cause us to press deeper and deeper into our relationship with God—to find His immeasurable love, and strength and peace. Only He will sustain us in the trials ahead.

# Introduction

In the spring of 1980 there were rumblings on Mount Saint Helens. For months there had been many minor eruptions of dust and ash. Even when the north side of the volcano started to expand ominously, setting up for the great explosion, many experts were still reassuring the public and TV viewers that there was small chance of a major eruption. This "reassuring view" was to some extent motivated by political and economic interests—the powerful logging industry wanted to continue its operations in the vicinity of the volcano. There were, however, dissenters to the "expert" point of view. This minority group believed that Mount Saint Helens showed all the signs of a volcano in its latter stages, ready to erupt at any time. As we all know, this group was vindicated a short time later when the mountain blew off its top. Unfortunately, this was little comfort to those who believed the "official view" and lost their lives by being too close to the mountain.

Today, our economic volcano is also expanding ominously. Debt upon debt, greed and covetousness, lifestyles far beyond our means, have brought about a veritable explosive situation

11

in this country. Our economic volcano has been building for years. It has often had minor eruptions of dust and ash: problems of the banks and Savings and Loans, third world debt, farm foreclosures, budget deficits, trade deficits, etc. It is ironic that some of the safeguards instituted in the Great Depression, to prevent financial panics, are now creating the ingredients for a new economic collapse and possible panic. Only recently has our economy moved into this very unstable ground. We are at the point where a major eruption and possible collapse in our economy and financial well-being could occur at any time in the foreseeable future.

There are many economic experts who are yet keeping the country asleep. They are like the prophets in Jeremiah's day who proclaimed, "Peace, peace," when the day of judgment was just around the corner. These economists continue to proclaim that all is well and safe despite the many problems. They contend that the government and the central bank have it all under control—no need to worry. Most of these economists hope for a "soft landing" (economic jargon for an easy way out without a severe recession). Many of these "experts" have an economic interest in keeping the public asleep, for they profit from peoples' investments. It is these lucrative but terribly mismanaged investments which have now brought us close to economic ruin.

There are other economists, however, who have seen the dangers of our gross lifestyle and economic misdeeds and have given ample warning of impending disaster. As recently as January 1987, the world famous economist John Kenneth Galbraith warned in Atlantic magazine about the speculative similarities between our economy and stock market and the economy and stock market of 1929. His words were vindicated just 9 months later when our own stock market crashed more than 500 points.

Alfred Malabre, economics news editor of the Wall Street Journal, writes in his book *Beyond Our Means*, "How America's

# Introduction

Long Years Of Debt, Deficits, And Reckless Borrowing Now Threaten To Overwhelm Us." He further writes,

> "For a very long time we've been living beyond our means—for so long, in fact, that now sadly, its beyond our means to put things right, at least in an orderly, reasonably painless manner . . . . No amount of governmental, or for that matter private, maneuvering will avert a very nasty time ahead."[1]

He likens our economic problems to a hurricane which has been brewing for many years. He states,

> **"It's my conviction that the next economic hurricane—the first to strike this nation since the Great Depression arrived in 1929—cannot be prevented. Its development is too far along."[2]**

Benjamin Friedman, economics professor at Harvard, writes in his book *Day of Reckoning*,

> "The thesis of this book is that the radical course upon which United States economic policy was launched in the 1980's violated the basic moral principle that had bound each generation of Americans to the next since the founding of the republic: that men and women should work and eat, earn and spend, both privately and collectively, so that their children and their children's children would inherit a better world. Since 1980 we have broken with that tradition by pursuing a policy that amounts to **living not just in, but for, the present. We are living well by running up our debt and selling off our assets. America has thrown itself a party and billed the tab to the future**. The costs, which are only beginning to come due, will include a lower standard of living for individual Americans and reduced American influence and importance in world affairs."[3]

He further states,

> "With no common agreement or even much public discussion, we are determining as a nation **that today**

13

should be the high point of American economic advancement compared not just to the past but to the future as well."[4]

More than 2500 years ago Isaiah brought the word of the Lord to Israel:

> *Therefore this iniquity will be to you like a breach about to fall, a bulge in a high wall, whose collapse comes suddenly in an instant* (Isaiah 30:13).

Israel had taken the blessings of the Lord and used them in an idolatrous and self-centered lifestyle. She chose to follow after other gods, while neglecting to show mercy and good works to those in need. Her society had become corrupt and unstable. The picture of a bulging wall was apt in its description of Israel's deterioration; natural attrition and God's judgment would bring its collapse.

Today our economic wall is bulging in America. Like Israel, our idolatrous lifestyle has led us away from the Lord. We have become as it says in II Timothy 3:2-4, *lovers of self . . . and lovers of pleasure.* In our own wisdom we have piled debt upon debt through economic mismanagement, as we have sought to maximize the experiences of this life. As a nation we have become like the prodigal son, taking our national inheritance and blessing and squandering them in just these last few years.

Our forefathers believed that all blessings came from God. Americans have all but forgotten this; most people believe that blessings are derived from our own ingenuity, education, and the institutions we have created. God is about to shake this bulging wall to show that much of America is built on sand and to show that much of what she stands for is rooted in the wisdom of man, not in the Word of God.

> *For the Lord of hosts will have a day of reckoning and the pride of man will be humbled . . . and the loftiness of men will be abased, and the Lord alone will be exalted in that day* (Isaiah 2:12a, 17).

# Introduction

Flight 232 with more than 270 people on board was on a crash course in the spring of 1989. One of its engines had blown out the hydraulic system, causing a near total loss in the control of the aircraft. The passengers were warned of the impending "hard landing" or crash, and in the remaining minutes they spent their time practicing crash drills and praying. When the plane crashed in a corn field, miraculously, over half the passengers survived. In a similar way, our economy is like flight 232. We too have lost much control of our nation's financial destiny and are likely headed for a "hard landing," maybe even a crash. We also need to take the appropriate defensive measures as God leads us, and we also need to spend much time in prayer.

Many would look at this book and say, "its another gloom and doom book." They would say, "tell us something good about our economy and country." Well, there are undoubtedly many good things to write about. However, the overwhelming evidence as this author sees it, is that we are on a crash course. Once the people on board flight 232 learned of the possibility of a crash, all other things which were not related to that possible crash became secondary. It is the purpose of this book to detail in a small way the spiritual and, in particular, the economic deterioration of our country and the reasons why a crash is very likely imminent.

This is not an investment book, as such, so there will be no word here on how you can invest your money in order to gain more wealth. (There will, however, be some discussion of financial matters in the chapter, Practical Considerations). Our problems are great and few will become richer in the times ahead. The riches that God is desiring in our lives are spiritual fruit—faith, obedience, love and good works. Only these will stand in the hard times and will build riches into eternal life.

We must always remember that God's judgment is meant to lead others and ourselves into a greater openness and receptivity to His mercy and His love. As in Psalms 103,

> *The Lord is compassionate and gracious, slow to anger and abounding in lovingkindness. He will not always strive with us; nor will He keep His anger forever. He has not dealt with us according to our sins, nor rewarded us according to our iniquities. For as high as the heavens are above the earth, so great is His lovingkindness towards those who fear Him* (Psalms 103:8-11).

I believe this book is a call from God to prepare for economic judgment on America, and through repentance and faith to thoroughly set our minds and hearts on things above—our Lord Jesus Christ. By the grace of God, these trials can enable us to grow more and more into the stature of the One who Loved us and gave His life for us.

# 1

# A Most Significant Sign

*But He answered and said to them, When it is evening, you say, "It will be fair weather, for the sky is red." And in the morning, "there will be a storm today, for the sky is red and threatening." Do you know how to discern the appearance of the sky, but cannot discern the signs of the times* (Matthew 16:2, 3)?

On October 19, 1987, the financial world was shocked by the crash on the stock market. The market dropped by more than 500 points (22% of its value) in less than 7 hours. Even the wildest of imaginations had not anticipated such a drop. Yet the crash was worldwide, affecting all the markets from America, to Europe, to the Far East. Many were puzzled. Why had it happened? Some thought there was too much speculation in the market and it was only a temporary correction or aberration which would soon be over. Others saw imminent recession on the horizon.

The stock market has always been one of the most reliable leading indicators for the economy. The leading indicators are a group of economic statistics which the Commerce

# Like A Bulging Wall

Department keeps track of and releases once a month in its *Index of Leading Economic Indicators.* This gauge has been very reliable at predicitng the future course of the economy. Generally, when the indicators rise for several months in a row, a stronger economy ahead is indicated. Conversely, when the indicators fall for three or more months, it usually signals recession ahead. The stock market itself has been the most reliable of all the indicators. It has been an accurate predictor of the future course of the economy 85% of the time. But historically, when the stock market has dropped an enormous amount as it did on October 19, 1987, it has been 100% accurate at predicting a very severe recession or depression yet to come. This recession or depression, however, does not appear instantly after a stock market crash. There is usually a time delay of several months to several years before the onset of this recession/depression. In 1929 the depression developed within a year of the crash, while in the 1870's it took about 4 years.

The stock market crash of 1987 (if we are to judge according to its accuracy) is predicting an economic downturn of deep pain and long duration. This downturn will probably not be driven by the normal recessionary pressures, but rather by the burden (and potential collapse) of our enormous "DEBT." It may be that this economic calamity, which even now is afflicting us, may be the worst in history and will result in the total revamping of our social, political, and economic structures.

The historical reliability of the stock market, as a "leading indicator," and the magnitude of the October 1987 crash should have brought caution to many people, especially those in business and politics. Initially, this was the case. But, when the feared recession did not begin as expected, many assumed the stock market crash was merely a jiggle in the statistics. Buying and selling, credit and debt, the economic world went back to its normal state. Many of our business and political leaders had indeed forgotten that there can be a significant time delay between a stock market crash of this magnitude and the resulting recession/depression.

In the most recent crash prior to October 1987, the crash of 1929, the economy fared quite well for a number of months after that crash. In fact the newspapers during the winter following the 1929 crash also spoke of the mildness of the recession and the hoped for belief that business could control any coming downturn from becoming serious. This was a vain hope, for the economy eventually followed the 1929 crash and became the Great Depression of the 1930's.

Often in the midwest we have strong thunderstorms. Sometimes you can see the storms approaching many miles away and hours before they actually hit. You can see the lightning, hear the thunder and feel the strong wind in your face. Once in a while there is an amazing calm just before the storm strikes, when the wind dies down and the lightning abates. This calm can be quite deceiving, causing one to believe for a moment that the storm has departed.

Concerning the economy, I believe that we have been in that calm before the storm. The stock market crash of 1987 was the first lightning strike of that coming storm. Since that time the stock market (with much speculation and takeover fever), has continued back to its earlier levels. The economy, too, has continued to prosper until just recently. This calm has deceived many into believing that either no storm of recession will come or else it will be quite mild when it does arrive. Yet the stresses in our economy, caused by our massive debt, not only have resisted improvement but continue to worsen. The storms of the coming economic crash are continually getting stronger and closer and even now are engulfing our economy.

*The simple believes everything, but the prudent looks where he is going. A wise man is cautious and turns away from evil, but a fool throws off restraint and is careless* (Proverbs. 14:15-16).

19

Will we be like the wise man who sees the danger ahead and prepares for it? Or will we be like the fool who in accepting the wisdom of the world, believes that prosperity will surely continue because someone else has it all under control?

## Stock Market Crash Reflects Speculation

Just as in 1929, the stock market crash of 1987 reflected the tremendous amount of speculation in our economy. The tax cuts in the early 1980's put an enormous amount of extra money into our economy. Much of that money went into the hands of the wealthy. No longer did they need to hide their income in tax shelters, because their top tax rates were lowered. Much of that money was undoubtedly used to play the market, invest in real estate, etc.

Also we saw great speculation in the 1980's in the business and corporate mergers, takeovers, and leveraged buyouts. This activity was largely promoted by the pro-business philosophy of the Reagan administration. Now, there is nothing wrong with being pro-business, however the real damage was done when the administration failed to control the excesses of the corporate takeover mania. The last time our nation saw this kind of corporate activity was—you guessed it, the roaring 1920's.

The stock market in the 1980's saw the rise of institutional investors via pension funds, insurance companies, etc. and computer program trading. Computers started to dominate the trading in the stock market. An institution might buy or sell millions of shares of stock in an instant when its computer tells it that it can make a few cents per share. No longer is the bulk of stock trading done to hold stocks for longer term profits and dividends. This kind of computerized institutional short term trading has made the stock market very speculative and volatile. The market can go up 40 points one day and come down 60 points the next. When all these short term traders and computers come together and reinforce themselves, you can have crashes as we saw in both October 1987 and October 1989.

The forces of increased wealth, of corporate merger and takeover fever, of pro-business government, and of institutional and computerized stock trading served to push the stock market to record highs in the 1980's. The stock market grew 250% in the latter 1980's. Contrast this with our economy which grew less than 25% during this same time period. The stock market's increase, therefore, did not at all reflect true economic growth. More than anything else it served to demonstrate the extreme speculation in this period of time.

Our stock market was not the only one which soared to new highs in the 1980's and early 1990. Markets all over the world experienced the same phenomena, some scoring much better gains than our own market. This only shows that extreme speculation in the financial markets is worldwide. That is why the October 1987 crash was worldwide and it is why the coming depression will also be worldwide.

Speculation in our country is not solely limited to the financial markets. Much of real estate has also experienced the same speculative increase—as investors have propelled the prices upward (this is especially true on the East and West coasts). Real estate, too, may be in for a fall.

Speculation is really quite rampant throughout our society. Consider the great increase in lotteries in almost every state. The driving force behind this and other kinds of promotions is the "get rich quick" mentality.

Therefore, the stock market crash of 1987 was not just a mere aberration or jiggle in the statistics, but it reflected the extreme speculation in the financial markets and also in our society. An economy which is heavy in speculative ventures is also an economy which is heavy in debt. This is because much of the speculation, especially in the financial markets and real estate, is done with borrowed money, via bank loans, junk bonds, pension funds, insurance, etc. Therefore, most of the financial and lending insitutions in our country are quite-tied-in to this extreme speculation.

**It is no accident, then, that a stock market crash is usually a precursor to a great depression.** The tremendous instability of a debt-heavy and speculative economy can easily come crashing down. The resulting liquidation process of this debt can take years.

The stock market crash in the fall of 1987 reflected the extreme imbalances in our economy, especially the tremendous government budget deficits, the trade deficits and the rampant speculation. Simply put, we have become a country living beyond our means—**the credit card society.** Our nation is like the person who, having lost his job or part of his income, refuses to face reality, but continues to borrow in order to support his current lifestyle. As Paul Volcker, former head of the Federal Reserve Bank, said repeatedly, "We are living on borrowed money and borrowed time."[1] The borrowed time comes because the borrowed money allows us to postpone the inevitable confrontation with reality.

The stock market crash of 1987 merely said in a strong way that "borrowed time" was coming very close to an end. The great imbalance in our economy created by speculation, borrowing and our lust for material things and pleasures, would soon come to an end. There might be a few more months of time left, but eventually our spendthrift habits, together with our lenders, will force us to bite the bullet. God will allow our nation (as blessed as it has been) to reap the consequences of what has been sown. All of us will suffer, not just a few. I am convinced, though, that through the hard times to come, God will bring many to repentance. He will cause many to see that the real riches are not to be found in the possessions of this life, but in the spiritual blessings of eternal life.

# 2

# The 1980's
# —Age Of Prosperity—

For most people who lived in our society in the 1980's, these seemed like "good times." We had no wars; the economy buzzed along for some 7 plus years; inflation was low (4-5%); employment was at record levels; gas prices were reasonable; and even our relations with Russia greatly improved. Consumer confidence was at record levels and President George Bush saw 70% approval ratings. In general, there was a cheerful feeling of euphoria in the land as the best times in 30 years seemed to be at hand. In the 1980's it was still quite possible to live the American Dream—to have a nice job, a good income and a big house. The following article from Newsweek entitled *The Fairy-Tale Economy, Is There Ever Going To Be Another Recession?* relates to this euphoria:

> "Maureen Allyn calls this 'the Goldilocks economy.' The chief economist at Scudder, Stevens & Clark, a big money-management firm, explains: 'Its not too hot and not too cold but just right.' **The economy is so perfect, she says, that there will be no recession for as far**

23

**out as she can forecast—through 1990.** But Allyn says there's one big problem with her scenario: 'Goldilocks is a fairy tale.' "

The article further states:

"The happy economic numbers continued to befuddle the experts. The current economic upswing began in 1982 and has continued for 81 months, a record for peacetime . . . . Some economists are beginning to entertain the heresy that the old boom-and-bust business cycle is dead. 'No recession ever? I'd never say never,' said John Taylor of President Bush's Council of Economic Advisers. **'But there's nothing automatic . . . there's no reason the expansion can't go on, well, indefinitely.' "**[1]

These last words of President Bush's economic advisor are quite similar to those made by a man named Irving Fisher, an economics professor at Yale. This man is most famous for his forecast of September 1929, when he said: "The world is now on a plateau of permanent prosperity." As we all know, that world crashed just a short time later.

I believe that these times of prosperity and euphoria are on the verge of ending, and the times to come will be in stark contrast to the age in which we now live . Few may be prepared emotionally, financially, or spiritually for the sudden changes ahead. The prosperity of the 1980's have left most of us like the disciples at Gethsemane, slumbering and sleeping and unaware of the dangers ahead.

For one to understand the deceptively "good times" we live in, it is necessary to review a little recent history. The 1980's began with twin recessions, one in 1980 and the other in 1982. In 1980 Jimmy Carter was running against Ronald Reagan for the presidency. Inflation and interest rates were both sky-high and threatening to scuttle the reelection of President Carter. In the winter of 1980 President Carter decided to put some restraints on credit borrowing in order to dampen the fires of inflation. Little did he realize that

## The 1980's—Age of Prosperity

America was hooked on credit like an addict hooked on drugs. The credit restraints caused our country to go into a severe tailspin and recession. President Carter was forced to lift the credit restraints after just a few months. The medicine was too bitter to swallow at that time, but a harbinger of times yet to come when America will be forced to take the medicine and live within its means.

Ronald Reagan won the election on the promise of balancing the budget in his first term. This was the very same promise President Carter had made 4 years prior and failed to achieve. However, in his first months of office President Reagan was to push through legislation which would totally scuttle any attempts at achieving a balanced budget. The cornerstone of this legislation was the massive tax cuts he gave individuals and businesses. This legislation came about because the President and his advisers had bought into a concept called "Supply Side Economics." This concept proposed that by giving tax cuts to individuals and corporations, enough new businesses and new taxes would be generated to more than offset the original tax cuts. The hope was that these newly generated taxes would eventually pay off the budget deficit.

Unfortunately, the practical application of "Supply Side Economics" failed miserably. After more than 8 years of tax cuts and much new business generated, the federal budget deficits are still out of sight. In order to finance these tax cuts Federal borrowing shot up from $50 billion a year to $150-200 billion a year. Perhaps these tax cuts would have been manageable if there had been a concomitant cut in government spending. However, after some small cuts the first year, government spending continued to rise throughout the 1980's. However miserably "Supply Side Economics" worked for our budget deficits, it did provide the rationalization for America to go on one last borrowing and spending binge and to continue living far beyond her means. Even though our country had been borrowing for years, "Supply Side" tax cuts acted like a giant credit card, pumping huge amounts of money into our economy.

The tax cuts of the early 1980's, more than anything else, helped to usher in the current times of prosperity. These tax cuts provided massive stimulation to our economy, pumping well over a trillion dollars of borrowed money into our economy these last 8 years. That money, together with the billions of borrowed dollars spent by consumers and corporations, has generated a lot of business and a considerable number of jobs in our economy. It becomes clear then that much of the economic prosperity and well-being that we have experienced these last few years is the result of these trillions of dollars of borrowed money being spent in the economy. Dr. Friedman states:

> **"By now it is clear that this sense of economic well-being was an illusion, an illusion based on borrowed time and borrowed money . . . . In short, our prosperity was a false prosperity, built on borrowing from the future.** The trouble with an economic policy that artificially boasts consumption at the expense of investment, dissipates assets, and runs up debt is simply that each of these outcomes violates the essential thrust that has always linked each generation to those that follow. **We have enjoyed what appears to be a higher and more stable standard of living by selling our and our children's economic birthright."[2]**

This kind of false prosperity ultimately has to end. There is a limit to the amount of debt that a people and a nation can borrow.

Normally, tax cuts especially those as large as we have had, are highly inflationary. These tax cuts, which increase the government's budget deficits, ultimately cause the Federal Reserve Bank to create "money." This newly created "money," which is used to pay off government debts, eventually causes all prices to move higher. The adage "there is no free lunch" is certainly true, because we pay for tax cuts eventually with higher inflation rates and the erosion of our income. This was especially true in the 1970's where relatively small budget deficits led to double digit inflation.

In the 1980's inflation has been noticeably absent despite the massive stimulation from the tax cuts and from individual and corporate credit spending. As it turns out, someone else has been picking up the tab for our "free lunch." The Japanese, Germans and others have been financing part of our borrowing binge. They have been investing their surplus earnings in our economy and purchasing our debts, knowing full well that our spending spree is a boom to their economies. This boom, however, has led to our other deficit, the trade deficit, where we annually spend $100-$200 billion more on foreign goods than they spend on our goods.

Throughout our history most economic expansions, i.e. times when the economy is growing, have lasted approximately 3 to 3½ years. These expansions have generally been longer in wartime and shorter in peacetime. However, in the prosperous years of the 1980's we have already set a record for the longest peacetime business expansion in our nation's history—more than 7 years. Normally, an economic expansion ends when higher inflation pushes up interest rates to the point where consumer spending (through credit purchases) becomes severely limited. When the consumer cuts back his spending, it forces businesses to cut back also, usually with layoffs. These cutbacks feed on themselves, ultimately producing a recession. While a recession is painful, it is not usually a "bad" thing for the economy. A normal recession helps to clean out many of the credit excesses generated from the expansion, and allows individuals, corporations, and banks to regroup and improve their balance sheets. This improvement in the balance sheets leads to less borrowing, less inflation, lower interest rates and ultimately a new business expansion.

One of the major reasons for the longevity of the most recent business expansion is foreign financing of our debt.

27

This financing has kept inflation low and taken the pressure off the Federal Reserve Bank to hike interest rates. With low interest rates the "borrow and spend spree" has been able to continue almost indefinitely. However, there is a big footnote to these amazing years of prosperity. History has shown that the longer the expansions go, the more severe the recession at the end. The severity of the recession is increased, because there is considerably greater credit excesses in a longer expansion which ultimately must be liquidated.

What a price to pay for prosperity! In the last decade our national debt has tripled to nearly $3 trillion. Our trade figures have gone from surplus to massive deficits as our "borrowed" affluence has sought and bought the goods from other countries. And finally the ultimate, **America has become the largest debtor nation in the world in just these few short years.** The Bible says, *and the borrower becomes the lender's slave* (Proverbs 22:7). In these few short years we have bought prosperity by selling ourselves into slavery. As far back as the mid 1980's Federal Reserve Chief Volcker said, "We need to get our own house in order and resist the temptation to being held hostage by foreign markets."[3]

Chief Volcher was of course referring to our rapid enslavement to foreign capital and their financial markets in order to supply the money needed to keep our economy in order. When the Japanese, Germans and others finally decide to cut off their export of financial capital to us, then our "borrowed time" will be over. We will be forced to live within our means. That time is evidently getting closer and closer.

Despite the very impressive, yet deceptively prosperous years of the 1980's, one has only to look below the surface to see the many problems which have accumulated because of our enslavement to debt. Our debt-burdened economy, like the "wall" in Isaiah's prophesy is bulging more and more as it continues to deteriorate. The 1980's saw the most massive foreclosure of family farms since the Great Depression. Many of these farmers had borrowed heavily in order to increase their equity and also profitability. These borrowers had not reckoned on the low crop prices of the 1980's and many of these farms ended on the auction block.

Starting in 1982 with the Mexican debt crisis and continuing throughout the 1980's there has been continuous news concerning troubles with loans to developing nations. The words "restructuring of loans," "writing off of debt," "moratorium on interest payments," etc., tell the story as our country and the world financial community have grappled with these "ticking time bombs." Many of these countries are close to defaulting on their loans, hardly able to make their interest payments. A new economic downturn will probably bring many of these loans into actual default, causing great problems for the money center banks.

Again, despite 7 plus years of economic expansion we read of continuous problems with our nation's financial institutions. Indeed, our banking institutions are weaker now than at any time since the Great Depression. In the latter 1980's hundreds of Savings and Loans had to be closed, merged and bailed out with an ultimate cost perhaps exceeding $500 billion. The most recent estimates predict that the cost will go much higher because many more S&Ls are sick and in poor condition. Furthermore over 1,000 commercial banks also failed in the last decade.

There are many other ticking time bombs in our economy such as leveraged buyouts, underfunded pensions, the insurance industry, budget deficits in all areas of government, trade deficits, etc. I will discuss many of these problems in the coming chapters, but it is sufficient to say that there will be great problems in this new economic downturn. Jesus said, *For if they do this when the wood is green, what will happen when it is dry* (Luke 23:31)? If we have had these great underlying problems in the "good times," what will it be like now that our economy is starting to enter the economic downturn. The "bulging wall" of our economy has great potential to crumble and collapse. The illusory peace and prosperity of our age can disappear in the blink of an eye. The dangers ahead are quite real and it is imperative that we turn to the One, the only One who has all the answers and can satisfy all our needs—Jesus Christ.

# 3

# Mountains and Mountains of Debt

Anyone visiting America in the late 1980's or early 1990's would truly marvel at the great abundance that seemingly is ours. Nearly 75% of our families own their own homes, with some of the newer homes similar to small castles. In the average house there are several telephones and TV's. The typical household owns 2 or 3 cars, and many teenagers have their own cars. Americans eat out more than one third of their meals, and the average person has excess weight from the abundance of food. During the summer months recreational vehicles, boats, and motor homes are seen almost everywhere, and many people go to their second homes on the lake or in the mountains.

We look at all this material wealth in America and thank God for His blessings. While it is true that God's hand of blessing has been upon our nation in the past, is the abundance that we now witness truly God's blessing? Much of the apparent wealth of this country is an illusion bought by mountains and mountains of debt. Is it a blessing to increase wealth by borrowing when God has made a clear provision against this in His Word (Romans 13:8; Proverbs 22:7; Deuteronomy 28:12)? It is borrowing and the resulting illusion of wealth which are now bringing our country into slavery. The mountains of debt have been growing at an ever faster pace recently and now seek to topple our country into economic depression.

It would be one thing if this apparent wealth and blessing which we see in America were largely the result of hard work, industriousness, and new inventions. To be sure, there is still much industriousness in our country. However, in recent years much capital and investment has been put into speculative ventures such as real estate, leveraged buyouts, consumer goods, etc., to the detriment of long term productivity goals, of research and of manufacturing. There is not the same exalted standard of living in Japan and in other countries where their production and investment in research are much higher than ours. In Japan, for instance, the average houses are quite small, many of them do not have heating, and about one fourth of the homes do not even have indoor plumbing. Yet the Japanese work 6 days a week, save 15% to 20% of their income, and prefer to make their purchases with cash, not credit. It is no wonder that Japan and other countries like it are rapidly assuming the role of world banker and lender, a position we held until just a few short years ago.

As I have said before, our high standard of living is largely based on our desire to live beyond our means and satisfy that desire through credit purchases or deficit spending. But you say, "I have not borrowed; how does that affect me?" Unfortunately, you do not need to be a borrower in our country to be affected. The national urge to live beyond our means through governmental, corporate, and personal borrowing is what is largely propelling the illusory prosperity of our country and giving you and many others a lifestyle and income significantly larger than you normally would have. In the decade of the 1980's our total debt load increased by approximately $6.3 trillion to a total of nearly $10 trillion. This is an astronomical increase! The federal government alone, largely through the tax cuts of the early 1980's, has technically given every family of four nearly $30,000 extra income in this decade. This is money every family would have possibly paid in taxes if the tax cuts had not been enacted. With all this extra money flowing in the system, it is no wonder that our lifestyle is far exalted over our world neighbors.

Your first response to the last few sentences is probably, "I sure didn't notice any increase in my income from these supposed tax cuts." If you made this response, you very likely are right. In an article in the New York Times, entitled, *Crux of Tax Debate: Who Pays More?* was written,

> "With the economic expansion of the 1980's, the wealthiest Americans saw their pretax incomes rise sharply while their tax rates dropped. The Reagan administration argued that tax cuts, by stimulating investment and expanding the economy would actually bring more revenue to the Government than less.
>
> According to a study by the Congressional Budget Office, after accounting for inflation, the top 5 percent of American families will have 45 percent more in pretax income in 1990 than they did in 1980. But the overall percentage they pay in major Federal taxes has fallen from 29.5% to 26.7%, a drop of almost 10%.
>
> Precisely the opposite trend occurred on the bottom of the income ladder . . . the poorest 10% of Americans will earn 9% less in 1990 than in 1980 and the percent of their income that they pay in taxes has risen from 6.7% to 8.5%, an increase of 28%.
>
> For the bulk of the middle class both pretax income and tax rates remained about the same, the budget office figures . . . the cut in income taxes and the rise in payroll taxes (social security) essentially cancelled each other out."[1]

33

# Like A Bulging Wall

For most Americans, the tax cuts were nullified by other tax increases. However, the wealthiest Americans and businesses received the biggest bonuses through these cuts. It is very likely that this increase in concentration of wealth in the top income groups has helped promote the extreme speculation in the stock market and in other financial areas. Indeed, Southern Methodist economics professor, Ravi Batra believes that this increase in "wealth disparity" is the major reason our country faces a coming depression. Dr. Batra wrote the book, *The Great Depression of 1990*, and he believes "the 1990's will suffer the worst economic crisis in history."[2]

Regardless of who received the money from the tax cuts, that money did get put into the economy via massive increases in the budget deficits. In the graph (page 35) one can see the enormous amount of deficit spending that has occurred in the 1980's. In this decade alone, our national debt has tripled to nearly $3 trillion. In 10 short years we accumulated double the debt that our nation took over 200 years to accumulate. Furthermore, our budget deficits are estimated by the Congressional Budget Office to explode to well over $300 billion in fiscal 1991 and 1992. This is an ominous trend indeed and points the way to ultimate bankruptcy in our national economy.

In the graph on page 36 one can see how the mountains of government debt have exploded in recent years. Unfortunately, this debt has served to destabilize our financial structures. We are like a ship which has gotten so top-heavy- the smallest storm can force it to flounder.

It is often stated by economists that even though our debt has grown, so has our economy. Therefore, they imply that we can afford more debt. However, the graph on page 37, which shows debt as a percent of Gross National Product, clearly indicates that debt has far exceeded the growth of our economy.

It may be a valiant idea to increase our country's defenses

# Mountains and Mountains of Debt

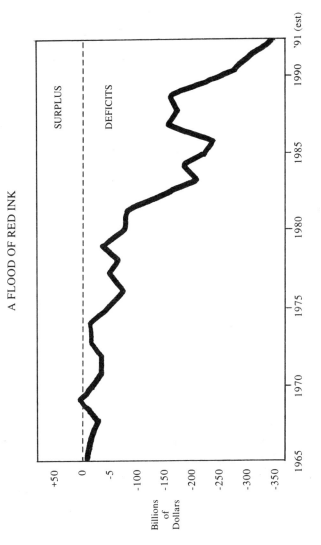

A FLOOD OF RED INK

SURPLUS

DEFICITS

ANNUAL FEDERAL BUDGET DEFICITS
Source: U.S. Office of Management & Budget

Billions
of
Dollars

35

# Like A Bulging Wall

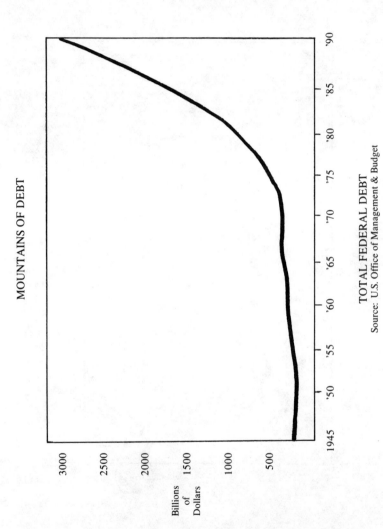

MOUNTAINS OF DEBT

TOTAL FEDERAL DEBT
Source: U.S. Office of Management & Budget

Billions of Dollars

# Mountains and Mountains of Debt

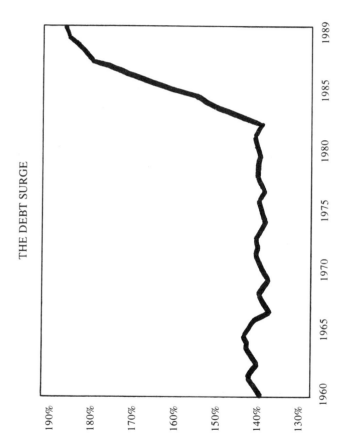

THE DEBT SURGE

Total U.S. Nonfinancial Debt as a Percentage of Gross National Product
Source: Federal Reserve Board

# Like A Bulging Wall

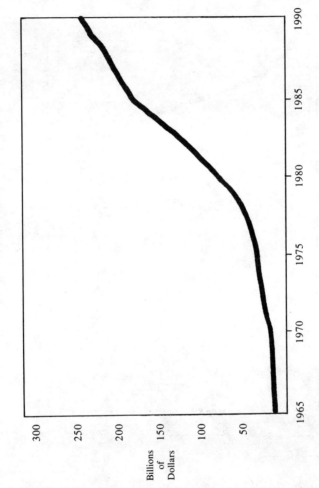

AN EXPLOSION OF INTEREST PAYMENTS

INTEREST PAID ON FEDERAL DEBT
Source: U.S. Office of Management & Budget

# Mountains and Mountains of Debt

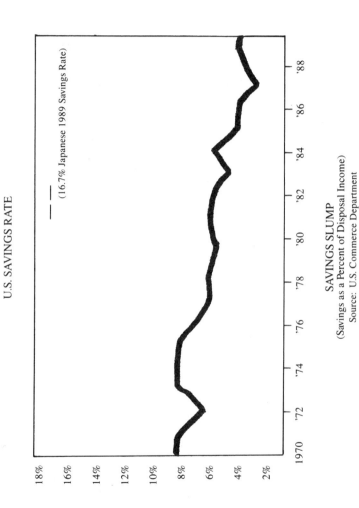

U.S. SAVINGS RATE

(16.7% Japanese 1989 Savings Rate)

SAVINGS SLUMP
(Savings as a Percent of Disposal Income)
Source: U.S. Commerce Department

with strategic new weapons, but it is the height of "insanity" to remove our economic defenses with heavy borrowing in order to achieve a false and temporary prosperity.

We have all heard of the miracle of "compound interest." Money left in a savings account generates interest on interest and this increases your money significantly faster. Unfortunately, "compound interest" works the same way with debt. This compounding has made interest payments on the Federal debt the fastest-rising component of government spending. The graph on page 38 shows the explosion of interest payments on our federal debt. These interest payments are now the second highest item on the government's budget, rising from $37 billion in 1976 to nearly $240 billion in 1990. Budget deficits could be eliminated if there were no interest payments, but this is impossible with $3 trillion in debt. Clearly, if the "compounding interest" trend continues with government debt, eventually a majority of the Federal budget will be used just to service the debt. This is precisely what has happened in some of the poorer nations.

Will the government ever work to get a balanced budget? A few years ago when the Gramm-Rudman bill was passed, there was hope that this bill might give government the needed discipline to get its fiscal house in order. This bill mandated automatic budget cuts if Congress did not reduce the budget by a set amount each year. Unfortunately, our government has virtually made a sham of this bill. In an article entitled *Critics say House Bill to Cut Budget Deficit is Mostly Hokum*, Charles Green has this to say,

> "Even in the Alice-in-Wonderland world of congressional budget-making, the 'deficit-cutting' bill now before the House is something special.
>
> The legislation is supposed to be Congress' annual exercise in fiscal responsibility. The bill's sole purpose is to reduce the budget deficit. But instead of cutting the deficit, the measure may wind up increasing it.

'I've never seen anything quite like this before,' said Carol Cox, president of the Committee for a Responsible Federal Budget, an independent watchdog group. 'In the long term, this bill will, without question, increase the deficit.'

Cox said the legislation is not surprising, however, 'I don't think anybody cares about the deficit right now,' she said. 'Congress has agreed with the administration that it is prudent for everybody involved to ignore the problem and pretend it's going away.' "[3]

Some of the so-called budget cuts include the following:

"The October payday of 2.1 million people in the armed services was moved up by 3 days to push $2.9 billion of deficit back to fiscal 1989 and out of 1990.

Savings of $470 million are being claimed by delaying payments to doctors under the Medicare program and shifting the burden to fiscal 1991.

About $1 billion in agriculture payments will be moved on the ledgers from fiscal 1990 to fiscal 1989."[4]

The list could go on and on. Unfortunately, this kind of fiscal irresponsibility by our government leaders suggests that budget deficits will never be corrected until there is a significant economic crash. Everybody talks about budget deficits but no one wants his benefits cut or his taxes raised. Tax cuts win elections, while those who promote sounder economic policies get defeated.

If only our federal and state governments were the ones plunging our country into debt, this would be serious enough. However, our governments are really no more than a mirror image of what is happening in the private sector. Government is only giving to the people that which they really want (more benefits without taxes). The average person has been pursuing his own desires and dreams, living beyond his means, with the same buildup of credit and debt as our government. Everywhere you go, the plastic card dominates. Americans owe an average of approximately $35,000 per person. In 1989 consumer installment debt (this includes all loans excluding mortgage) was well over $700 billion, roughly 45 times higher than the 1950 level; and mortgage debt was about $3.5 trillion, over 45 times its 1950 level. Consumer installment payments at one time used to take 5-10% of income, but now have risen to a record 21%.

Again, the negative part about the growth in consumer debt is that it leaves a person with little margin of error when the next recession comes. Strapped for payments on charge cards, car loans, and house payments, the average person is not equipped to sustain any real income loss due either to wage cuts or job loss. Furthermore, the illusion of wealth may give the person a false security and prevent him from preparing for hard times. The end result could be default or bankruptcy.

## Drop In Savings

The great increase in debt has paralleled another dangerous trend in our society: Americans are saving less and less. Savings are the lifeblood of a nation. Savings provide the capital and finances needed to provide for growth in research, manufacturing and productivity. Without adequate capital we lose our competitive edge in the world economy. The trade deficit is hard evidence that we are indeed losing this edge. As mentioned earlier, our foreign investors often save 18% of their income, and until the 1980's Americans were saving approximately 8% of their income. However, in the 1980's the savings rate has consistently dropped, hitting a low of 3.7% in 1987. The graph on page 39 shows the seriousness of this savings decline, happening at the same time as our debt load is massively increasing.

Traditionally, savings have been seen as a nest egg. This nest egg served as a means to save for the larger things one wanted to purchase, and as a hedge against the uncertainties of life. However, the illusion of prosperity and the widespread trust that government will take care of all needs (be it medicare, social security, unemployment payments, etc.) has caused many to draw out their savings, borrow, and go on a spending spree. This has left many vulnerable to the waves of the coming economic downturn. We are like the 2 pigs in the story of the *Three Little Pigs.* We have been busy building our houses of sticks and hay—all too complacent that the wolf has gone elsewhere to live.

The psalmist wrote,

> *I will lift up my eyes to the mountains; From whence shall my help come? My help comes from the Lord, who made heaven and earth* (Psalm 121:1-2).

The psalmist was challenging the pagan view which looked to the hills and high places as a means of help rather than God Himself, who made all creation. The hills and mountains that our country is trusting today, those institutions and creations of man, are full of debt and so highly unstable that they threaten to bring our country to its knees. Only in returning to the God who made heaven and earth will we find our help. As Christians we need to get our house in order, and as Jesus commanded, "to watch and pray." For the American economy may be close to crashing and He would not have us slumbering and sleeping.

# 4

# How Did We
# Get Into This Mess?

The roots of our problems are as old as mankind. Nevertheless, many of our current problems (at least economically) began during the last great economic crisis, the Great Depression. During the 1930's a new concept was unleashed as a means to pull this country out of the Great Depression. It was called deficit spending and it eventually had far-reaching consequences on our whole way of life. Basically, the idea was simple—the government would use borrowed money to try to stimulate a depressed economy. Deficit spending was needed, the reasoning went, because economic conditions in the 1930's caused most people to tighten up on their spending and become savers. Many people were out of work and those that did have work did not have assurance concerning the future of their jobs. In the 1930's the government did not provide unemployment benefits as we now have and social security was in its infancy. Most people then chose the time-honored way of facing uncertain times: they saved their money.

# Like A Bulging Wall

Cutting back on spending and saving more does slow the economy as it did in the 1930's; however savings eventually builds a nest egg which can be used for future spending. This spending is released when people feel enough confidence in their jobs and in the future of the economy. Ultimately, the economy of the 1930's would have returned to normalcy, but the Roosevelt administration was under enormous pressure to get the economy going and going quickly. Deficit spending was justified as the means to pour money into the economy, because the people were unwilling to spend and consume. Government would spend the money that the people were saving. New social programs, public works projects, farm crop price supports, etc. were launched in an effort to spend the borrowed money and hence stimulate the depressed economy.

Deficit spending, while a new concept for our country, was rather ineffective in pulling our country out of the Great Depression. It wasn't until World War II, with its great demand for men and weapons, that we finally pulled out of the depression. The government borrowed (especially with war bonds) and spent massively during the war years. Most of the unemployed found jobs, either on the front lines or in the war factories.

When the war ended in 1945, the United States was clearly out of the depression. It was also in the enviable position of leader of the "free world" and creditor to many nations rebuilding their war-torn economies. Our people had saved much during the war years, and now that it was over they started to spend some of that money on new houses, cars and appliances. In 1946 Congress enacted the Full Employment Act, pledging all government resources to keep America fully employed. Again, this seemingly innocuous act showed the direction our government was heading—a direction which would ultimately employ massive government deficits in order to keep our economy rolling.

After the war it was feared that we would enter into another depression once the massive stimulation of war-time spending ended. The depression never materialized for the nest egg savings which the people had built up in the 1930's and in the war years was now gradually spent on many items that Americans had been deprived of. The spending was gradual in the years after the war; although there was no boom, business gradually increased on a solid footing. Government also was conservative in the late 1940's and 1950's and refrained from deficit spending. It even managed to pay off some of the prior debt during those years.

When the 1960's began, a real shift was evident in American life. The shift was towards the philosophy of "secular humanism" and in particular "selfism." Whereas concepts such as "duty," "responsibility," "self-sacrifice," "industriousness," "love of God," "love of country," and "honor" had motivated our country for nearly 200 years (concepts which directed us away from self), the new shift was evident in the narcissistic question, "What's in it for me?" Books, professors, and counselors all started to emphasize the need to live for "self" and to satisfy one's own needs first. Fritz Perls, founder of Gestalt Psychology, made a statement that reflected the attitude of the times; "You do your thing and I'll do my thing and if by chance we meet, that's great." "Self actualization" and "self realization" became the catch words of this new movement. No longer was it seen as "in" to live for God, or family, or country and to put another's needs ahead of one's own needs. In fact it was told that such actions might damage or at least restrict one's personal growth. To be true to one's self and do what feels good in your own eyes was fast becoming the primary emphasis during this time.

Everything in society began to reflect this move towards self-centeredness and self-preoccupation. Novels, movies, and music all began to move in a more sensuous direction, as they emphasized the need to satisfy the pleasures of self. Forgotten were the admonitions of the Bible:

47

# Like A Bulging Wall

> *Do not be deceived, God is not mocked; for whatever a man sows, this he will also reap. For the one who sows to his own flesh shall from the flesh reap corruption, but the one who sows to the Spirit shall from the Spirit reap eternal life* (Galatians 6:7-8).

> *For whoever wishes to save his life shall lose it; but whoever loses his life for My sake shall find it. For what will a man be profited, if he gains the whole world, and forfeits his soul? Or what will a man give in exchange for his soul?* (Matthew 16:25-26).

As our nation indulged more and more in the thoughts and sins of the "flesh," even God was proclaimed to be "dead." It wasn't that God was dead, but that man's spiritual life had become dead. For the newly proclaimed freedom and liberation of the self-life was in actuality suffocating the "spirit" and man's communion with God. As Paul said,

> *For many walk, of whom I often told you, and now tell you even weeping, that they are enemies of the cross of Christ, whose end is destruction, whose god is their appetite, and whose glory is in their shame, who set their minds on earthly things* (Phillipians 3:18-19).

As America came ever more into the bondage of "self" and the pleasures of the "flesh" in the 1960's, 1970's and 1980's, the "works of the flesh" (which Paul enumerates in his epistles) became increasingly evident. Crime, divorce, sexual perversions, pornography, murder, abortions, homosexuality, witchcraft, and sorcery (as evidenced in the New Age movement) all became rampant in our society. Even worse were the rationalizations given to many of these "works" as the logical outcomes of this new "liberation." Adultery and immorality were seen as "sexual activity." Homosexuality was seen as an alternate lifestyle. Abortion was seen as a woman's choice. Rock music, which earlier generations of missionaries had witnessed in demon-possessed tribes, was seen as the free expression of youth.

48

## How Did We Get Into This Mess?

What was seen in earlier generations as "gross sin" had now become readily acceptable and recognized as "normal behavior." There are so many examples in our society of the deteriorating "works of the flesh" that it is dangerously easy to become lukewarm and complacent. One can go to a variety store nowdays and see books showing all kinds of suggestive and immoral behavior on the covers. One can watch the news on TV at night, only to be interrupted by some immoral or violent scene from an upcoming series. Perhaps one can venture into a video store to obtain a "wholesome family movie," only to find nearly every movie polluted by profane language and sexual exploits. The list illustrating the deterioration of our society could go on and on.

I am reminded of the experiment with a frog in hot water. If the water temperature is raised suddenly, the frog becomes quite aware of his changing environment and jumps out. However, if the temperature of the water is raised slowly, the frog becomes increasingly lethargic and sleepy until it no longer can jump out—and it dies. Many of us have become like the frog in the experiment. We, too, have become increasingly lethargic and sleepy in a society which has been slowly but steadily deteriorating. Many of us have become imbued with the false peace of our apparent prosperity. We have the same false confidence that the world does, namely that government and the various institutions of man will ultimately be able to protect us from all evil. We need to be reminded and awakened to those words of Galatians 6:8 again. The sins of the flesh do not only lead to things getting worse but ultimately to destruction. We are indeed closer to judgement than we think. We need to call upon God in repentance for the sins of our nation and of ourselves.

Perhaps more than any other of the "sins of the flesh," the sins of greed and covetousness, have captured our society. It is these sins, perhaps above the others, which now seek to topple us into economic judgment. Everywhere in our society we are exhorted to "buy," "buy," and "buy." In a thousand different advertisements we are told that our self image, our success and, of course, our life fulfillment depend on buying many, many things. Is it any wonder that people are constantly dissatisfied with the things they have, especially those that age and lose their appeal?

Nearly 30 years ago when the philosophical shift toward humanism and selfism began, another idea was also making a comeback. The idea went something like this, "Why not enjoy the things you want now—you don't need to save, you can pay for it later?" This surely sounds like the words of the tempter leading a people into slavery. The idea neatly fit in with the explosion of advertisements which began to bombard the American public. In conjunction with this idea the credit card was promoted. The credit card became the easy way one could impulsively satisfy all those real and imagined needs which advertisements had created. Credit card purchases have so progressed that nearly 70% of department store purchases today are through credit. An even larger percent of credit purchases are made for big ticket items, such as appliances, furniture and autos. Contrast this with the people of Europe and Japan who are loath to use the credit card and are encouraged to save rather than consume. Small wonder they are becoming the world's lenders.

During the 1960's, secular humanism and selfism developed the rationale for living according to the desires of one's self, whereas the credit card provided the means for working this out in everyday life. At the same time that the credit card was being unleashed for personal use, government also decided to get in on the act. Deficit spending, which hadn't been used much since World War II, was reborn. High sounding social programs, such as War on Poverty, etc., were launched in order to spend this borrowed money. (Later the Vietnam War was also to take its share of this money). One of the major reasons for deficit spending, however, was to stimulate the economy into higher states of growth, more prosperity, and of course more votes at election time. In this respect government also was reflecting the philosophy of secular humanism. By giving the people more prosperity than they normally would have without deficit spending, government was indirectly promoting the false views of self realization/actualization. By giving a false and elevated sense of affluence, it encouraged people to think more highly of themselves. This action in turn became self-reinforcing. For when people think more highly of themselves, they often tend to increase their purchases (especially with credit).

Likewise, many businesses decided to throw "caution to the wind" during this time and get their "piece of the credit pie." Increased debt was taken on as a means to boost expansion and to maximize profits. Short term profits, especially in quarterly reports, became the obsession rather than concern for the long term growth and health of the company. Again the same attitude dominated: "get the most out of life now."

Alexander Paris states how government deficit spending had the effect of changing business attitudes,

> "First, government spending and the resulting deficits financed by the Federal Reserve served to stimulate the economy. Second, the management of the business cycle through fiscal and monetary policy eliminated many of the natural corrective forces of the cycle, which had served in the past, to moderate the rate of increase in the growth of credit. Finally, the success of limiting the extent of any economic corrections, together with the rhetoric by government and economists regarding the demise of the business cycle, served to create a climate in which individuals **changed their credit ethic and corporations and banks changed their business approach.**"[1]

This change in ethic which was promoted by government deficit spending and government "guarantees," was the point where things started to deteriorate. Mr. Paris states again,

"The growing belief that serious business recessions had been eliminated, also led to the belief that much of the business risk had been eliminated or in the case of banks particularly, shifted to government. This led banks to feel safe in reducing drastically the size of the buffers once thought necessary to protect against risk of deposit withdrawals . . . . The same attitude led corporations to feel comfortable with lower levels of liquidity and with debt-heavy capital structures."[2]

Deficit spending and government guarantees became an artificial stimulant to pump extra growth into our economy. Alcohol and drugs are also stimulants and we know they have an effect on a person's perspective of reality. They can cause a person to set aside his morals and engage in behavior he would not normally do. Deficit spending, easy credit and government loan guarantees also tended to change the perspective of our people, businesses, and banks. It tended to blunt their normal cautions and ethics, and to encourage more reckless financial decisions. Ultimately, this would lead to the tremendous banking and financial crisis which now looms over us.

During the 1960's, then, deficit spending increased dramatically not only on a governmental level but also corporately and privately. All this extra money produced the intended prosperity, for we had the longest economic expansion in history. Inflation and higher interest rates eventually pushed us into a nasty recession in 1970. Three years later we were again brought to another severe recession in 1973. These recessions, although bad, did help to wring some of the excesses from the economy and bring some balance back in the credit markets. Unfortunately, our society was now hooked on "credit" like an addict hooked on drugs. No longer could people get by with postponing and saving up for purchases as our forefathers had done. The cry of a people hungry for material things easily drowned out the remaining constraints.

## How Did We Get Into This Mess?

"We must have it now, or we will go where they will give it to us," became the general voice. Thoughts of the future, whether they be national, societal, or spiritual, took second place to the impetus to maximize life "now."

Businesses also became totally and dangerously dependent on the "credit drug." Retailers needed the credit to keep customers coming to their doors. Businesses needed it for continued expansion and also to service their ever burgeoning debt load. Government, too, could no longer balance its budget, for the benefits it had promised our people were too great and the economy was too dependent on the massive stimulation of deficit spending. Ultimately, debt becomes a "drag" on economic growth, and higher and higher levels of economic stimulation are needed in order to achieve the same amount of growth. It is much like an alcoholic who finds he needs ever larger doses of liquor in order to get the same "kicks." As the debt levels got greater and greater in our society, we were forced to increase deficit spending in a like manner in order to achieve the same level of growth.

Debt, then, became the dangerous drug which allowed us to live out our fantasies and to buy things which former generations would have done without. Spending borrowed money serves the pleasures of the "flesh" and gives the false sense that one is in control of his life. Furthermore, credit purchases can become the ultimate in pampering oneself, especially with luxuries that one could not normally afford. Credit purchases, whether it be a car, house, furniture, trips, etc., can foster the idea that we are somehow "better" than we actually are. This in turn creates a false lifestyle which forces one to become dependent on credit purchases in order to maintain a particular image. Like a person on drugs, our society has largely been unaware of the growing bondage of credit spending.

The 1970's, like the 1960's, continued the trend in our society of credit spending and debt accumulation. By the end of the decade, inflation and interest rates were double digit, and this credit or deficit spending chased prices ever higher. Interest rates peaked at 21% and brought us into the twin recessions of 1980 and 1982. These recessions were painful, but they were reminders that pain and judgement are the end results of this kind of living. Before these recessions had time to bring our country and economy back into balance, we were again back to administering the "credit drug." "Supply Side Economics" was used to justify one more large massive dose of the "drug," causing our national debt to more than triple in the last decade. This massive dose was to provide a gigantic tax break while hardly cutting any federal programs. It has done the trick! The massive dose of deficit spending has fueled our economic boom for over 7 years.

The drug of credit spending, however, is about to wear off. Over 6 trillion dollars of credit spending (by all sectors) in the 1980's has created a grandiose and illusory lifestyle. Our economy is tragically like a stack of cards or a house built on sand. When the rains of recession/depression come (as is now the case), much of our economy may come tumbling down. Our lenders may not be kind or generous and will surely force us to pay our bills.

# 5

# Our Tragic Trade Deficit

Perhaps one of the most striking symptoms of our economic malaise is the development of the trade deficit. More than anything else the trade deficit is the outcome of living beyond our means on borrowed money. We are literally borrowing from the world in order to buy their goods.

For nearly 65 years our nation has been a net lender to the world, and we have continuously exported more to others than we imported from abroad, i.e. we had a trade surplus. It is no coincidence that our ability to lend to others, especially after World War II, propelled us to the position of world leader. Our lending helped build war-torn economies and made the dollar the currency of the world, i.e. the currency by which other nations value their money. This position as "world lender" allowed us to score many favorable trade advantages with other countries.

Starting in 1982, our balance of trade literally began to collapse. We no longer exported more than we imported, as the chart on page 56 clearly shows. Furthermore, we became

55

# Like A Bulging Wall

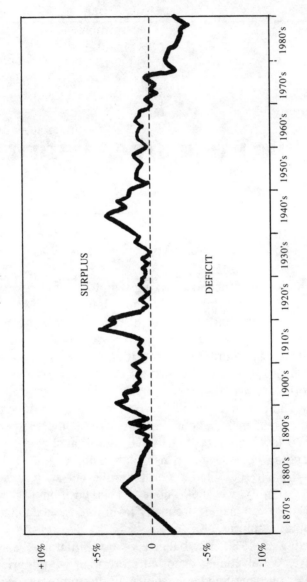

U.S. TRADE BALANCE
(Now A Debtor Nation)

SURPLUS

DEFICIT

Trade Balance as a Percent of Gross National Product
Source: U.S. Commerce Department & Economic Indicators

dependent on foreign money in order to finance our appetite for foreign goods. By 1985 we had become a debtor nation, something we had not seen since the beginning of this century. Our net investment position in the world, a surplus of $149 billion which took us 65 years to accrue, was squandered in 3 short years. By 1987 we became the world's largest debtor nation, passing countries like Brazil, Argentina, and Mexico.

How did the trade deficit and our progression to debtor nation status happen? Again, we find that our nation's urge to live beyond its means is the chief cause of the trade deficit. In particular, the massive tax cuts of the early 1980's, which caused our budget deficits to mushroom, was probably the primary mechanism for creating the trade imbalance. These budget deficits increased the borrowing needs of government significantly, thus forcing interest rates higher than normal. These higher "real" interest rates attracted foreign investors who could not get as high a return in their own countries. Foreign investors are no different anywhere in the world. They will go where they can get the highest return on their money, and the fact that we have a stable political system also helps.

So, foreigners were attracted by our interest rates in the early 1980's. However, in order to purchase our bonds and government securities, they needed to purchase dollars first. They did this by exchanging their own money for the dollar, but this pushed the value of the dollar to record heights by 1984. While a stronger dollar enabled us to purchase foreign goods more cheaply, it also caused our goods to be more expensive on overseas markets. During the early to mid 1980's, the dollar increased in value by some 64%. Prices of foreign goods fell by more than 20% while the prices of our exports increased by 12%. Benjamin Friedman explains what happened to our industries,

> "The collapse of our international competitiveness during the first half of the 1980's was spectacular in both speed and extent. One industry after another, labored

under an increasing overvalued dollar, withered before the forces of foreign competition—cars, motorcycles, bicycles, steel, textiles, shoes, electronics, TV's, radios, personal computers, telephones, lawnmowers, etc. Since early 1985 the dollar had fallen sharply but by 1988 our trade had only begun to recover. There is no guarantee that the market shares lost by American firms at home and abroad, or the jobs lost by American workers in industries exposed to ruinous international competition when the dollar was so sharply overvalued will readily return."[1]

Living beyond our means via the budget deficits caused our dollar to become overvalued on exchange markets and allowed foreign competition to crack our markets with cheaper imports.

During the mid to latter 1980's, the dollar fell on exchange markets due to the supply of dollars in circulation and because of lower interest rates. However, despite some improvement in our trade figures, the trade deficit remained stubbornly high. The fact remains that we have lost much of our competitiveness in world markets. While we have been content to spend our savings and capital on bigger houses, cars, boats, shopping centers, etc., our international competitors have been putting their capital into bigger and more efficient factories, tools, machinery, research, etc. We have been eating our "seed corn" these last few years. Rather than thinking and planning and building for the future, we have been all too eager to live and spend and borrow for the "NOW." The trade deficit is the barometer for what we have lost in world competitiveness.

We also have become dangerously dependent on foreign credit to supply our overconsumptive lifestyle. By 1986 foreigners held some $476 billion of our bank deposits, $415 billion of our treasury securities, $209 billion in our real estate, and $167 billion in our stock market. They continue to pump nearly $150 billion per year into our economy, a good portion financing the Federal budget deficits. As a result of this foreign financing the Federal Reserve Bank has not been forced to monetize much of the budget deficits, i.e. to finance them by creating money. This, however, has left our central bank in a very difficult position. If it tries to lower interest rates too much, foreign funds might leave our markets causing the dollar to drop and wreak havoc. If the Fed keeps interest rates too high, it could create a recession which also would undermine foreign investment in our "debt." Either way, we have become dependent on our international investors to eventually set our policy.

Our overconsumptive lifestyle has literally been financed like a home equity loan. In a home equity loan a person gives back some of the equity in his home in order to secure the loan he desires. In the case of our country, foreigners are increasingly using their excess dollars (which have piled up through the trade deficit) to buy our real assets. Dr. Freidman states,

> "Foreign investors who may become nervous about holding deposits issued by U.S. banks and securities issued by the U.S. Treasury are perfectly free to buy up our businesses and our real estate instead. As we shall see, they are already doing so in increasing volume, and given the vast amounts of dollars held abroad, it is clear that the process has only begun. We are surrendering the ownership of our country's productive assets, not in exchange for assets we will own abroad, but merely to finance our **overconsumption**. The realization that we increasingly live in foreign-owned buildings and work for foreign-owned firms, once it dawns, will jar harshly with our traditional perception of America as a nation of owners."[2]

He further states,

> "The balance against us, already amounting to more than $7,000 per family, now makes the U.S. the world's largest debtor. **Foreigners have already begun to settle these debts by taking possession of office buildings**

in American cities, houses in American suburbs, farmland in the heartland and even whole companies. We are selling off America and living on the proceeds."[3]

One half of the commercial real estate in Los Angeles, one third of that in Houston, and one fourth of that in New York City are now foreign owned. In New York City alone Japanese companies have paid $610 million for the Exxon building, $250 million for the Mobil building, $175 million for the ABC building, and $670 million for part of the Citicorp building.

Besides real estate, foreign investors have been increasingly interested in purchasing and controlling ownership in a number of companies. A number of recent company mergers and buyouts have been from foreign firms. For instance, Nestle, which is Swiss-owned, bought Carnation; Unilever, which is Dutch, bought Chesebrough-Ponds; Hoecht, which is German, bought Celanese; Bridgestone, which is Japanese, bought Firestone. There have literally been hundreds of other such mergers and buyouts like the ones mentioned above.

The question arises, "What difference does it make who controls America's businesses?" Foreign ownership or control of our companies may not make any difference in the efficiency of our companies (some may even be helped). However, increasingly, business decisions will no longer rest with the people of this country. Furthermore, the profits generated by these companies will no longer return to our people through dividends, but will increasingly go out of this country to enhance the wealth and power of other peoples and nations. Instead of our traditional role as a nation of owners, we will become a nation of tenants, having sold off our assets and businesses in order to finance a lifestyle beyond our means. As Esau sold his birthright for a pot of stew, so we are selling our national assets to keep the party going.

Besides losing control over our own productive assets, our trade deficits and our new status as a debtor nation will ultimately reduce our influence in the world of nations. Historically, countries that have been lenders have been able to exercise much world leadership. Great Britain ruled the high seas in the 17th and 18th centuries not only because she had a mighty navy but also because she was a great lender. After World War I, Great Britain's power dwindled when she ceased to be a lender. Her power became even more reduced after World War II when she became a net borrower. Dr. Friedman states,

> "One worrisome implication of America's becoming a debtor nation is simply our loss of control over our own economic policies. **Losing control over one's affairs is, after all, what being in debt is all about—no less for a nation than for an individual or a business . . . .** Over time the respect, and even deference, that America had earned as world banker will gradually shift to the new creditor countries that are able to supply resources where we cannot, and America's influence over nations and events will ebb."[4]

Today we are still leader of the free world, but this is largely due to the work of our forefathers and the grace that God has bestowed on this country. Our creditor nations which have helped support our overconsumptive lifestyle during that last few years have not yet evicted us from this favored nation status. However, eventually the bills will come due and our lenders may not be so kind, especially if we go into a recession/depression. If we have trouble servicing our debt, we may be put in the awkward position (like other debtor nations) of having our affairs, especially our financial affairs, supervised by some international agency. As farfetched as this sounds, we too may be put on an "austerity budget" and be forced to balance our budget, increase our exports, and pay ourselves less wages. This has been the plight of other "debtor" nations, such as Argentina, Mexico, Brazil, etc. Ultimately, we may lose some degree of our sovereignty in the process, making it far easier for us to slide into a one world government.

## Like A Bulging Wall

The trade deficit is indeed a major symptom of our economic malaise. First, it shows that our economy, buoyed up by deficit spending and overconsumption, has been buying much more from the rest of the world than the world is able to buy from us. In fact, much of the world is either bogged down by excessive debt (as in the developing nations) or has had rather sluggish economic growth (as in Europe). In many cases these nations do not buy our goods, either because they cannot afford them or they choose not to use "credit." We are the engine driving the world economy, but alas we are also driving ourselves into debt and ultimate slavery.

Secondly, the trade deficit shows us that we have lost a good share of the competitive edge in technology and manufacturing to other countries. The other industrial countries have been spending much more of their Gross National Product on increasing their competitive edge. Alfred Malabre says this about us,

> "The problem isn't so much under-investment in general as under-investment in facilities that provide not instant rewards, such as a new houes, but longer-term benefits, such as a new factory. We have tended to over-invest in quick gratification."[5]

We have been content to pour more of our money into projects that satisfy present needs but do not build for the future. We have been borrowing and throwing ourselves an extravagant party. (If you don't think it is extravagant then you only need to compare our living conditions with those of almost any other country in the world.) While we party, many other major nations have been building up their productive resources such that they are now beginning to overcome us with their technological and financial might.

# 6

# Is It God We Trust— Or Is It Insurance?
## (the cause of the S&L crisis)

Recently I saw an advertisement on TV which painted a vivid picture of our country's situation. The picture showed a man holding the hand of his son and looking off towards a mountain. While they are gazing at the mountain, a deep voice assures them that they can trust all their needs to the "rock." The "rock," as we know it, is a well-known insurance company and the ad distinctly shows how pervasive is our trust in "man" and his financial creations. There is nothing wrong with financial planning or having a certain amount of insurance, as long as we keep our primary trust in God and not man. However, many in our society have long ago abandoned their trust in God and have replaced it with trust in man, in government and in insurance. It is this false trust which has created much of the problem now looming over us.

Our forefathers did not so readily place their trust in "man" nor in his financial instruments. In fact, our money still displays the words, "In God We Trust." It is no coincidence these words are on our money. Our forefathers knew that money and the lust for money corrupts and causes us to place our security in that which is not secure. Every time we look at money, it is to remind us to keep our trust in God. Indeed the Bible declares that God alone is our "rock." The psalmist states,

> The Lord is my rock and my fortress and my deliverer,
> my God, my rock, in whom I take refuge . . . (Psalm 18:2a).

It was in the Great Depression of the 1930's that insurance came to have much more importance in our nation's financial affairs. As a result of the many bank failures in that period, the Federal Deposit Insurance Corporation (FDIC) was formed. Member banks contribute to this insurance fund, which in turn protects depositors of banks that fail. At first the FDIC protected depositors up to $2,500 in their bank accounts, but this was gradually increased to the current $100,000 protection.

The FDIC and later its sister, FSLIC for Savings and Loans, were basically set up as a safety net to protect against an occasional bank going under. However, the psychology behind the insurance was far more important. It was meant to convey the message that now there was something solid behind the banking system. Insurance and ultimately government were behind the banking system. There was no need to become afraid of one's deposits in a particular bank, no matter how badly the bank was managed. This psychology worked! It stopped the run on the banks in the 1930's and has continued to prevent runs on the banks ever since. The psychology has continuously been working these last 55 years. Over and over it has been repeated, "the banks are perfectly safe, not a penny has ever been lost in an insured bank account."

Why then should we be suspicious of something like the FDIC or FSLIC, when they seemingly have done much good? First of all, the FDIC and FSLIC do not have adequate funds to protect the banking system. The FSLIC is already bankrupt, and Congress has had to appropriate billions to bail out failed Savings and Loans. The more sound FDIC fund has approximately $9 billion to protect deposits of roughly $2 trillion. This means approximately 1/2% of depositors' funds are in fact protected. If two or three large banks went under simultaneously, it would wipe out the entire FDIC fund.

How close is the insurance fund to going bankrupt? In a recent news article titled *More Bad News for Banking, S&L Industries*, the following was written:

> "Just when you think America's savings and loan disaster can't get any worse, it does. And now the insurance fund that covers deposits in the nation's commercial banks may be poised to plunge over the same cliff.
>
> Even more ominous, the General Accounting Office is 'very concerned' that the Federal Deposit Insurance Corporation—which guarantees deposits up to $100,000 in federally insured banks—may not have enough money left to honor its guarantees because big banks are so squeezed by regional real estate recessions, another GAO official warned.
>
> Richard Fogel (assistant U.S. comptroller general) conceded that if four or five major banks were to fail, that 'would deal quite a blow to the FDIC fund.'"[1]

We may not be far away from the collapse of the major bank insurance fund. In another article, *Good Idea Gone Sour: Can Bank Insurance Fail?*, Law Professor Jonathan Macey states:

> "The collapse of the savings and loan industry is already the most costly regulatory failure in the world. But even as that crisis unfolds, another is looming: Federal insurance of bank deposits, once considered an American birthright, may now be a luxury we can no longer afford . . . . In fact banking experts are now predicting the imminent collapse of the insurance fund that backs the commercial banking industry. Commercial bank

failures are on the rise while the FDIC's losses are at
an all-time high, and their loss reserves at near record
lows. **The bankruptcy of the FDIC's insurance fund
would be a body blow that even the resilient U.S.
economy could not withstand. Economic collapse
could ensue.**"[2]

It will only be a matter of time before the FDIC Insurance
fund is exhausted. Once the fund is used up, it will be necessary for Congress to appropriate additional money to pay
off depositors. This is precisely what has happened with the
hundreds of failed Savings and Loans and the bankrupt FSLIC
insurance fund. Congress may ultimately spend $500 billion
on the bailout.

The average person probably reacts to the news of the
bailouts by an "ho hum." I'm sure the question comes up,
"who cares about insurance or the banks as long as they get
bailed out?" However, these bailouts have occurred in basically
"good" economic times when Congress can afford to be
generous. Consider that the government has over $5 trillion
of loans which it is guaranteeing. This is a $20,000 per person
bill if the whole loan program needs to be bailed out. Would
Congress be able to fully bail out a banking crisis in deep
recessionary times, when its own deficit is expanding and it
has literally hundreds of commitments all asking for help?
In such times would our foreign creditors allow us to make
such a bailout while their own loans go unpaid? No one knows
the answer for sure, but my guess is that Congress may not
be able to afford the price tag for a major bailout in dire
economic times.

Since it is obvious that the insurance funds are way
underfunded and cannot provide adequate protection in severe
economic times, insurance psychology, rather than insurance
itself, is primarily the means protecting the banking system.
It is this psychology which convinces people that their funds
are totally safe if there is a FDIC or FSLIC sticker on their

bank's windows. Even though this psychology has held for nearly two generations, it could easily evaporate in times of severe crisis. This crisis could develop when first, the insurance funds become bankrupt (as already in the FSLIC) and second, when Congress is unable to fully repay all deposits. "A breakdown of the insurance machinery would be the financial equivalent of nuclear catastrophe," says Albert Wojnilower, chief economist of First Boston Corp., and "no individual acting alone can do anything to prevent such a disaster or to protect himself against destruction."[3] Indeed, once that psychology is broken, we could again see runs on the banks. Even worse than this, panic could spread to many other financial areas where the psychology of insurance has lulled many into complacency. Ultimately, insurance and the complacency it breeds spreads excess in the entire financial system. It is these excesses which threaten us with economic calamity; this will be discussed later.

Insurance and its psychology then have been working their course for nearly six decades and have nearly permeated every aspect of our society. Government guarantees are now standing behind an awesome $5 trillion of loans, including bank loans, student loans, farm loans, FHA loans, international loans, etc. Unfortunately, insurance psychology has created a deadly complacency in our society. It has created the attitude among Americans, and even among Christians, that insurance and ultimately government have it all under control. This author has questioned many people concerning whether America could ever enter another depression. In most cases the answer has been "no." Why is this? Most people believe that government through its various agencies, including the Federal Reserve, knows how to steer the economy so as to avoid calamity. God has a way though of shaking things up to see whether things are built on rock or on sand.

In the weeks and months before the 1906 earthquake in San Francisco, the city had finished a lavish building program.

# Like A Bulging Wall

Many municipal buildings had been rebuilt or remodeled with beautiful arches, columns, etc. The buildings were impressive enough, but after the earthquake a startling discovery was made. These buildings were the first to fall, and closer examination revealed that many of the structures were only hollow shells. The contractor had decided to increase his profit margin by building structures that were little more than facades.

Many of the financial structures in our society may be like those buildings in 1906 San Francisco. These are the financial structures to which most people are trusting their financial future. Ask most people about their future and they will enumerate their pension funds, bonds, IRA's, mutual funds, stocks, life insurance, annuities, and social security. These are financial instruments which we still call "securities." Many of these seem quite impressive, some having billions of dollars in assets. However, like the buildings in San Francisco, many of these financial pictures of stability, may be found to be only hollow shells, having dissipated their assets on high risk worthless ventures. In a New York Times article, *Insurance Analysts Worry That Crisis May Be Brewing,* Nathaniel Nash writes,

> "Concern is mounting among public officials and analysts that a financial crisis is brewing in the insurance industry.
>
> Losses are growing, though they are still modest compared with the entire industry's assets. But federal and state government officials are warning that a number of problems could combine to create a **significant crisis**, including a lack of adequate state regulation, low levels of capital, excessive risk taking . . . , weak managements, and evidence of illegality . . . .
>
> The industry holds a large portion of junk bonds issued by corporate America as well as large portfolios of real estate. Analysts argue that these assets are particularly vulnerable to an **economic downturn**, and that significant

> losses are already embedded in the value of assets on insurance company books."[4]

Although this article was written about the insurance industry, much the same has been written about other financial institutions. Many of our insurance companies, pension funds, mutual funds, and banks have invested America's savings in the great debt structure of this society—one that is highly leveraged and highly vulnerable in an economic downturn. Even more disturbing is the fact that many of these financial institutions have gone after the high risk "junk bonds" with a passion. Junk bonds are debt obligations which yield high interest rates because they are extremely risky. These bonds, which are given the lowest of credit ratings, are often used to purchase "leveraged buyouts."(These are companies like Nabisco, Pillsbury, Northwest Airlines, etc. I shall say more about these high risk buyouts in the next chapter.) Most junk bonds are a fairly new creation—coming largely from the takeover and merger mania of the 1980's. Most of these bonds have never been tested by an economic downturn, and many will probably not survive when one comes. So, why then are our trusted financial institutions investing in what others call "junk?"

Because junk bonds are quite risky, banks are prohibited by law from purchasing them. Nevertheless, many banks have gotten around this prohibition by lending money directly to the parties involved in "leveraged buyouts" (LBOs). Until recently, the largest banks in our nation had been making approximately 70% of their commercial loans to these high risk corporate mergers and leveraged buyouts. Of the $25.07 billion leveraged buyout for the giant food company Nabisco, bank loans provided nearly $14.5 billion. These loans would have to be classified as "junk loans" on the same par as "junk bonds." Now you and I would probably never take our life savings or our retirement funds and invest them in the riskiest of investments. Why then are some of the largest banks and financial institutions doing just this? The following Barrons' article, *Banks Are Borrowing Trouble With Loans To LBO's*, attempts to give an answer,

> "What's the explanation for the (banks) lemming like rush to LBO's (leveraged buyouts), given their recent bad experience with LDC (loans to developing countries) debt. It seems that individual bankers are often quite intelligent at assessing individual risks, but when the herd instinct takes over, the banks in aggregate, seem incapable of truly assessing the likelihood or impact of macroeconomic shocks."[5]

Again, in the same article insurance is seen to play a major role in allowing the banks to take such risks.

> "Federal deposit insurance was invented when the word 'prudent' was a code word for particular types of financial behavior. Now with the thrift industry run amok, and then aground, it is time to examine the appropriateness of insuring bank deposits based on the amount of money that will be insured as opposed to considering how and for what purpose that money is lent. The Savings and Loan bailout is now estimated at $100 billion, a high price for incompetence. The purpose of federal insurance for bank deposits was to **protect creditors, it was not to insulate banks from the consequences of ill-conceived lending practices.**"[6]

The article concludes with this word,

> "It all comes down to this: LBO's are risky and that's why they provide potentially higher rewards, but banks are rushing headlong into LBO lending with no guarantee to the government insurers that they are being any more prudent in their approach to LBO's than they were in their approach to LDCs."[7]

The reason these banks and financial institutions take such risks with your money is primarily because of the false security of insurance protection. Henry Kaufman, former chief economist of Salomon Brothers Inc., had this to say,

## Is It God We Trust—Or Is It Insurance?

"The various deposit-insurance arrangements, which seemed laudable in the 1930's, have served lately to remove the link of responsibility between creditor and borrower—the upshot is a world of unrestrained credit growth."[8]

Because of insurance protection then, it is no longer necessary to satisfy depositors with safe and sound investments. Profits become the dominant motivation. With so much money under insurance protection ($5 trillion), the capacity for huge excess is obvious.

It is nearly unheard of in the present time for one to open a bank account, or to buy an insurance policy, or to start a pension plan and ask to see that institution's investment portfolio. Very few people have any concerns about the security of their investments. One bank, or one pension fund seems as good as another, since insurance and ultimately the government are protecting the investments. There are regulators who are supposed to watch over insured financial institutions, but they have become fairly lax in recent years. They have allowed banks to lend money to just about anybody, and for any purpose. Insurance protection and a laxness in standards has produced the kind of mentality which allows big banks to lend money to underdeveloped countries with zero chance to repay—and to lend money to high debt, high risk companies in mergers and buyouts.

Actually, the problems with the banking industry began long before the current problems. The false security of insurance protection made it easier for banks and Savings and Loans to not only make riskier investments but also to mismatch the maturities on their investments. Banks and S&L's borrow money for different time maturities and they lend that same money out for different time periods. Ideally, these maturities should be matched—that is longer term loans should be matched with longer term deposits, and shorter term loans should be matched with shorter term certificates of deposit.

# Like A Bulging Wall

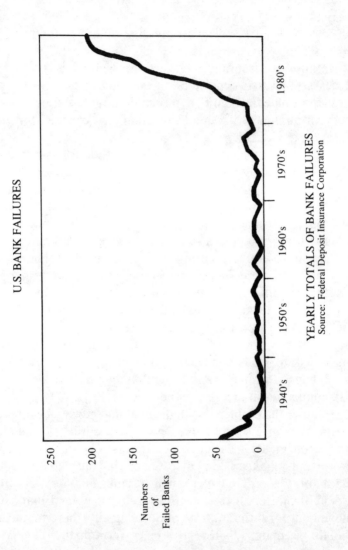

U.S. BANK FAILURES

Numbers
of
Failed Banks

YEARLY TOTALS OF BANK FAILURES
Source: Federal Deposit Insurance Corporation

## Is It God We Trust—Or Is It Insurance?

Matching the maturities of their deposits with the maturities of their loans means that a bank or a financial institution is liquid and solvent and can meet depositors' withdrawals on a timely basis. However, with our current banking system, mismatching maturities has been the norm for a long time. Banks borrow money on a short term basis in order to pay out the lowest interest rates, while they lend out money on the long term in order to get the highest rates. By borrowing short and lending long, banks and S&L's can increase their profit margin substantially. This practice, however, makes these financial institutions extremely "illiquid"—unable to handle even a moderate amount of withdrawals by depositors. Harry Browne in his book, The Economic Timebomb, states,

> "A bank with mismatched maturities is an illiquid bank.
> It never has the liquid assets to satisfy all the depositors
> who could demand payment. The bank is vulnerable to
> any event that might lead to greater than expected
> withdrawals."[9]

Banks and S&L's are primarily relying on insurance protection rather than "safe and sound" investments to protect themselves and their depositors.

We currently have a banking system which is quite "illiquid," fragile and carrying a portfolio of vulnerable investments. These investments have pushed the bank failure rate (as shown in the graph on page 72) to the highest levels since the Great Depression. Needless to say we are ill prepared for the next economic downturn.

One of the biggest examples of current bank weakness and also misuse of government insured funds is the Savings and Loan crisis. That crisis, involving the bailout of possibly 600 S&L's, dominated the news in the latter 1980's. The estimate of the government bailout which was first put at $50 billion may eventually rise to $500 billion. Many of these failed S&L's were located in the southwest and California where they were involved with energy loans and real estate. However, no areas

73

of the country were exempt. There are nearly $400 billion in assets from these failed institutions which must be liquidated. These assets, which have come from loan defaults, include shopping centers, apartment complexes, office buildings, homes, condominiums, and businesses.

The Savings and Loan fiasco, although partly caused by dishonest managers and loose regulators, was still in large part caused by money managers seeking to maximize profits at the expense of "safe and sound" investments. One of the largest S&L's to go broke was The Vernon Savings and Loan in Vernon, Texas. Ninety six percent of its loans went bad at an estimated cost of 1.3 billion dollars to taxpayers. This kind of loss is another flagrant example of the severance of responsibility between lenders and borrowers caused by the false security of insurance. Such a bailout is truly amazing for it occurred in "good" and "prosperous" times. What will transpire now that the economy is going down?

Hundreds of years before Christ, when Israel was being menaced by the armies of Assyria, Isaiah prophesied,

> For thus the Lord God, the Holy One of Israel, has said, "In repentance and rest you shall be saved, in quietness and trust is your strength" (Isaiah 30:15).

However, Israel was not willing to trust in God. Instead she decided to seek help from the arm of man—in the nation of Egypt. Isaiah again prophesied,

> And you said, "No, for we will flee on horses," therefore you shall flee! "And we will ride on swift horses," Therefore those who pursue you shall be swift. One thousand shall flee at the threat of one man, you shall flee at the threat of five; until you are left as a flag on a mountain top, and as a signal on a hill (Isaiah 30:16).

America, like Israel of old, is trying to find salvation in the arm of man rather than in the "God We Trust." Insurance protection and its psychology are some of those false and hollow gods to which we have given our trust—in the hopes of saving us from our predicaments. A sticker which states "Deposits backed by the Full Faith and Credit of the U.S. Government" will not save us. Our nation is now the largest "debtor" nation! These human instruments have in many ways made our situation worse and will ultimately not be able to deliver. We, too, may be left like a flag on the top of a hill.

# 7

# The Undermining
# Of Corporate America

Throughout the latter 1980's corporate activity made quite a few headlines, but much of it was not good. In the area where I live, I read numerous articles regarding locally based companies. A few generalizations of these articles will suffice:

> Pillsbury (which was bought out by Grand Met) was selling subsidiaries and laying off hundreds of workers in order to pay off debt.

> Honeywell was selling its Weapons Division, laying off hundreds, and buying back its own stock in order to prevent any takeover attempts.

> UNISYS (a takeover of Sperry by Burroughs) was planning to layoff hundreds in order to shore up profitability.

> Northwest Airlines (bought out by Al Checki) increased its debt load (through the buyout) so that it was no longer second lowest in debt of the airlines, but second highest.

These are just a few of the many examples repeated all over the country largely caused by the frenzy of speculative

# Like A Bulging Wall

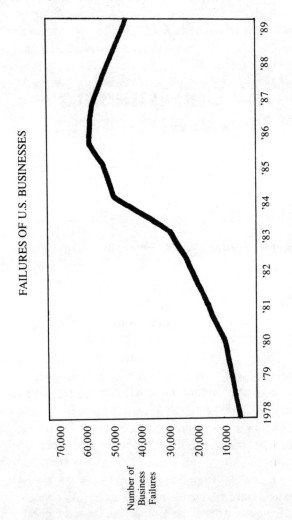

FAILURES OF U.S. BUSINESSES

Number of Business Failures

70,000
60,000
50,000
40,000
30,000
20,000
10,000

1978 '79 '80 '81 '82 '83 '84 '85 '86 '87 '88 '89

YEARLY TOTALS OF BUSINESS FAILURES
Source: U.S. Commerce Department

buyouts and mergers which gripped our country in the 1980's. These buyouts and mergers, commonly called "leveraged buyouts" (LBO's) reached their zenith at the end of 1988 with the $24 billion buyout of Nabisco. That buyout was financed with $19 billion of junk bonds and loans and has resulted in the selling off of numerous divisions and the laying off of hundreds of employees.

This kind of speculative activity found in corporate America in the 1980's has not been seen since the 1920's. It has resulted in the tremendous proliferation of corporate and business debt. Unfortunately, this speculation and accumulation of debt has severely weakened many businesses and will add to the seriousness of the next economic downturn. The chart on page 78 clearly shows the exponential weakening of our businesses in the relatively prosperous years of the 1980's.

Dr. Friedman writes concerning these business failures,

> "That these failures and defaults have taken place in a time of economic expansion raises serious questions about what would happen in the event of another economic contraction, which would again slash earnings and depress asset values. Business bankruptcies would probably increase substantially further; perhaps even enough to threaten the economy as a whole."[1]

Again, as I have mentioned many times in this book, if we have had this many failures in the "good times," what will it be like now that economic times are getting tough?

Our corporate history with debt goes back long before the speculative 1980's. The door to debt (as I have discussed earlier) was opened in the 1960's when deficit spending was revived not only as a means to solve many social problems but also as a means to propel our economy towards continuous growth. Deficit spending had the effect of causing many to believe that the business cycle with its ups and downs was eliminated. Acting like a drug it changed people's sensibilities. Caution and prudence were put aside. Alexander Paris states,

"With the growing faith in never-ending economic growth without serious business corrections and in the cult of earnings growth, it was only natural that corporations would turn increasingly to financial leverage to raise their rates of growth or to revitalize sagging growth. Little attention was being paid to the static balance sheet . . . . If the company could grow on its own capital, couldn't it grow even faster on others' money?"[2]

"Leverage" then became the new method of operation for many businesses. "Leverage," taking on of increased debt in order to expand business acitvities and increase profits, is not to be confused with the "normal" amount of debt which is generally required for business activities.

Earnings and profitability did expand in the 1960's as we witnessed an expansion of close to 9 years. However, the debt burden came to weigh more and more on companies, and in the 1970's our economy witnessed some very severe recessions. Economic expansion in the 1970's was termed "stagflation," indicating relatively poor economic growth with high inflation. Due to increased debt, companies found they needed to allocate more resources to service the debt. In the 1950's and early 1960's interest payments took only 16% of corporate earnings. In the 1970's interest payments took 33% of earnings and in the 1980's interest payments took a whopping 56% of earnings.

Higher debt loads and interest payments have left many companies today "cash poor." In the 1950's and early 1960's companies on the average could pay off all their short term debts, i.e. debts due within 1 year, with their available cash and bank deposits. However, in the 1980's companies on the average had less than 20% of available cash reserves in order to pay off short term debt. If business conditions worsen and cash flow becomes negative, most companies' short term debts would overwhelm their cash reserves in about 50 days.

We see then that U.S. businesses, increasingly straddled with debt and having little cash reserves, are working with very little margin of error. As long as times remain fairly good, many of these companies can marginally survive, especially if they have access to continued borrowing. However, in times of economic downturn many of these companies may flirt with "Chapter 11" bankruptcy. Our corporate history these last 30 years has generally gone from strength to weakness (even though there are many exceptions). We have leveraged off our strong assets as we have become more expansive, yet we have become weaker companies laden with debt.

As bad as our corporate debt situation was in the 1960's and 1970's it has markedly worsened in the 1980's because of the speculative mergers and leveraged buyouts. A leveraged buyout occurs when a person, group of people, or a company attempts to purchase another company's stock (its ownership) with borrowed money. The leverage comes because the buyers use very little of their own money to make the purchase. Its like the leverage of buying a house with 5% down and the rest from the bank. In the case of leveraged buyouts (LBO's) the purchasers usually get their money from the sale of junk bonds and from junk loans. The largest leveraged buyout to date was bought by the Kraus group with $5 billion of their own money and $19 billion in junk bonds and loans. The sale of these lowly rated bonds has skyrocketed in recent years. In the mid 1970's there was only about $10 billion of these bonds in existence. However, by the end of the 1980's their total had grown to over $200 billion. The sale of these high risk bonds has certainly helped to propel the current speculative mania. It is these junk bonds, with their high interest rates, which have attracted the buying of many pension funds and insurance companies.

Once a company is purchased through a leveraged buyout, the new owners often attempt to sell assets and streamline the company in order to reduce the level of debt and increase profitability. Nabisco and Pillsbury, recent LBO's, have sold off major divisions and laid off hundreds of employees in their efforts to reorganize and cut their debt.

81

## Like A Bulging Wall

Some would argue that leveraged buyouts are really not that bad for corporations—that they actually help to increase efficiency. While it is true that a company's efficiency may be initially helped, in the long run its balance sheet is hurt by the accumulation of massive debt. Senator Lloyd Bentsen, chairman of the Senate Finance Committee had this to say,

'Congress may be asked to bail out numerous corporations that will be forced into bankruptcy in the next recession because of excessive debt.'

A study showing a **spectacular increase in the amount of high risk "junk bonds"** debt since 1980 makes him worry about the possibility of a taxpayer bailout similar to the multibillion-dollar rescue of the nation's troubled Savings and Loans.

'The Library of Congress study tells us that the amount of corporate debt is going through the roof and that the quality of corporate debt is going through the floor. **When we see another recession—and ultimately we will—you're going to see that recession deeper and longer because of debt.** You'll see so many of them going bankrupt that you'll begin to hear cries for having the taxpayers go in and bail them out like we had to do on the Savings and Loan industry, and that gives me deep concern.' "[3]

We do not have to wait until a recession to see that troubles are already brewing in the highly leveraged companies. In an article entitled *Even in Smooth Seas, Some Takeovers are Going Under,* Washington Post writers Steven Vise and Steven Mufson make these comments;

"An outbreak of defaults by debt-burdened companies are sending the first shock waves through the world of leveraged buyouts and corporate takeovers. 'Leveraged buyouts are going bust like never before,' said Mary Bechmann, a partner in Corporate Development Associates, a fund that invests in troubled companies . . . . In the first half of 1989 there were $3.2 billion in defaults of junk bonds, more than double last year's pace.

The problems are even worse than they appear on the surface, according to Bechmann, who said that 'for every highly visible company struggling to meet interest payments, there are scores of others looking for help before they are forced to disclose their problems to the public . . . .'

Many financial experts have been surprised by the magnitude of the recent failures, given the overall strength of the economy.

**'The scary thing is we haven't had the recession yet, and these puppies are rolling over,'** said Ted Stolberg, a partner with the investment firm of Weiss, Peck and Greer. **'God help us when the recession comes.'** "[4]

The takeover mania has caused our economy to become paradoxical in the 1980's. A company like Northwest Airlines, which was strong and had good earnings and low debt, became an easy takeover target. At the same time, a company which has poor performance and high debt—is literally ugly—will often escape the clutches of the takeover artists. Unfortunately, the "scare of takeover" has forced many companies to take drastic measures. They have been forced to borrow money, buy back their shares—or fight the "raider," and to literally make themselves ugly or unattractive in the takeover market. The same article by Vise and Mufson makes these comments,

"Some of the companies now having financial difficulties were not involved in leveraged buyouts but used junk bonds to finance growth. In addition, the threat of takeovers has frightened many once-conservative companies into loading up on debt. To fight hostile suitors, these companies have borrowed heavily . . . ."[5]

Unfortunately, the defensive maneuver of taking on more debt, while perhaps helping prevent a takeover, severely weakens a company's ability to survive hard economic times.

# Like A Bulging Wall

Consider a company like Gilette, which used to be a company with low debt load and a solid balance sheet. After several fights to prevent hostile takeovers, this company has lost much of its cash reserves and has had to increase its debt load to well over 1 billion dollars in order to remain independent.

Again, the negative part about the takeover mania of the 1980's is that it has greatly increased the debt load of many companies, and it has caused others to lay off hundreds of employees. Furthermore, all those hundreds of billions of dollars which have gone into takeovers have not benefited the economy very much—especially in the areas of research, productivity and manufacturing gains. Most of this money has gone to increase the wealth of a select few.

In a recent Wall Street Journal article we see how the effects of this increased debt are now affecting companies. Notice the headlines:

## MANY FIRMS FIND DEBT
## THEY PILED ON IN THE 1980's
## IS A CRUEL TASKMASTER
### They Now Yearn for Equity As They
### Slash Expenses, Plead with Bondholders—
### LITTLE SYMPATHY FROM BANKS

"Even before a recession hits, the financial screws are tightening on many heavily indebted companies. Facing huge interest and principle obligations, **they have fallen captive to debt,** changing priorities to make ends meet and, increasingly, pressing banks and bondholders for relief . . . . 'They bet on the come,' (hunch that they're right) says R. Daniel Evans, president of Fitch Investors Service, the bond-rating agency. But as cash flow slows and financing alternatives evaporate, 'One by one we are watching them get into trouble.'

> But legions of executives who piled on debt in the 1980's, whether to buy out shareholders, pay special dividends to thwart a takeover, or acquire other companies, are realizing their chances of repaying it are slipping away—and could dwindle further in a recession. Already, corporate interest expense as a percentage of total costs is **higher than during any expansion in the past 50 years.** (Note the graph on page 86 showing this trend.)
> 'Companies don't have the luxury in a downturn to hold on to as many workers and undertake as much capital expenditures as before,' he adds. **The belt tightening 'will deepen the unfolding slump' in the economy,** he predicts."[6]

The article predicts that there will be approximately 150 companies having trouble making interest payments in the next few years and that there may be up to $69 billion in defaults in the next 3 years. I believe those estimates are very low because they do not take into account the severity of the coming recession/depression.

One company (as an example among many) that has experienced significant problems with its debt load is Forstmann & Co. Forstmann is the largest domestic manufacturer of woolen and worsted fabrics for suits. Forstmann took on heavy debt when it was acquired by an investment group in December 1988. Since that time suit prices have risen, causing men and women to put off purchases. Now Forstmann's cash flow is barely able to cover their $15 million annual interest. The company has been forced to cut its workforce by 600 people (20%), and greatly trim expenses. This is just one more example of what it means to be in bondage to debt, and it will get worse.

Why doesn't the government restrict or eliminate these leveraged buyouts? While there has been considerable talk

# Like A Bulging Wall

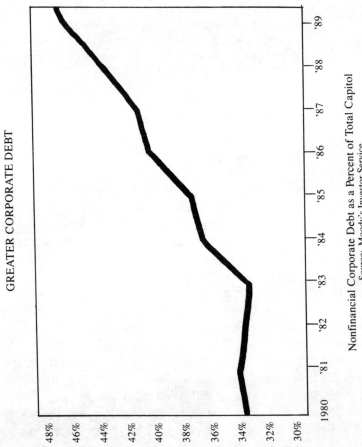

GREATER CORPORATE DEBT

Nonfinancial Corporate Debt as a Percent of Total Capitol
Source: Moody's Investor Service

on capitol hill about the dangers of leveraged buyouts, unfortunately, there are investment bankers, lawyers, and managements who are making millions on these deals. These people have considerable influence in government and obviously an enormous stake in keeping the takeover game going. Until there is a crisis of considerable magnitude, Congress probably will not act.

In years past a company raised capital, i.e. money to begin or expand, by selling shares of stock. The shares of stock were literally ownership or equity in that company and signified that those who were running the company were willing to share ownership with their shareholders. When times were prosperous and there were good earnings, the company would share these profits with shareholders in the form of a dividend. This was the long range program which helped bring our country into economic greatness. In this method of ownership there was a natural protection against hard times. When hard times came and earnings fell, a company could withold some or all of its dividends. The shareholders' lost profit would in turn help the company's cash position—which would substantially help it to weather economic downturns.

In the 1980's we saw a reversal of these trends that helped make our country great. Companies borrowed money in order to buy back their own shares of stock. This was termed by some as a "flight from equity" and was (as I've already discussed) caused largely by takeovers and defensive measures against such takeovers. It was also encouraged by our tax laws, where interest expenses are deducted and dividends are taxed. There still are companies who raise capital by selling stock, but the 1980's was the decade where considerable stock was replaced by debt. In the 7 plus years of the latest economic expansion some $585 billion of equity was retired and debt was increased by roughly $1.14 trillion. Contrast this with the Japanese whose companies are continually able to raise billions and billions through stock offerings. It is no wonder

87

they are fast becoming world leaders in the free market. Dr. Friedman states;

> "The massive substitution of debt for equity in conjunction with the onset of record high real interest rates has sharply raised the debt burden for the average American business."[7]

This pattern is truly ominous and shows again our movement from independence to slavery.

Back in the 1800's and in many parts of our world today, farmers had to battle hoards of locusts. In our economy the locust plagues are not in farming but in the business world where the takeover artists are ravaging our companies and causing many to go deeper in debt. In replacing their equity with debt, our companies have chosen in the short run what looks like a more profitable course. However, in the long run most of these companies will find "debt" a much harder taskmaster than "equity." When hard times come, and they surely will, many of these companies may have difficulty making interest payments. Whereas with stock ownership a company can suspend dividends, with debt a company can only suspend interest payments when it is forced into Chapter 11 bankruptcy. This may well be the course for many companies who have chosen to add debt upon debt in the speculative 1980's.

# 8

# A Possible Scenario

Look at our economy and the information that I have presented these last few pages, then look to the future. There are undoubtedly a number of possible scenarios that could unfold. Here I will present a scenario which I feel is most likely, but I am not a prophet or seer and events could unfold in a radically different way. Although some of these events may seem farfetched or frightening, we, like the passengers on Flight 232, need to be prepared for the worse. If God spares us some of the agony of these events, or even postpones them for a while, then we will thank and praise His Name.

The stock market crash of 1987 was, I believe, the warning call to the dangerous times yet ahead. The crash as we have already noted was partially caused by a lack of confidence that America would ever get its financial house in order. Since that time the economy has continued to purr along, and there have been some small improvements in the trade and budget deficit. This has probably helped to postpone the inevitable crunch. Although the stock market has returned to its original highs, it is my belief that there will be another crash of confidence sometime in the not too distant future. The stock market will be hit again, because it has a history of reflecting future economic trends and any lack of confidence that might arise. The new crash may not be as sharp as the October 1987 crash, but it will not be over in a couple days either. In fact, this new market crash could be a very slow downward spiral. The new crash may start in the Japanese stock market, which has been even more speculative. If the Japanese market gets hit, they may panic and pull their money out of other international markets. This of course would easily bring our market down, too.

The new crash will likely signal that our economic expansion (era of prosperity) is about over, and the painful readjustment of living within our means is about to begin. This new downturn will undoubtedly begin like other downturns, with rising unemployment, falling Gross National Product, business failures, and the like. However, because of the massive buildup of debt in our society, this downturn could easily snowball into greater severity. Heavily leveraged and heavily indebted firms and individuals will have difficulty making interest payments. Many of them may go under, and the effect will ripple through our economy, weakening other companies and financial institutions. Perhaps some large banks may fail, causing an ever increasing credit crunch.

In past recessions interest rates usually fell because demand for credit eased and the Federal Reserve Bank was able to supply more funds to the banking system. Interest rates may indeed fall in the early stages of the new economic downturn, but as the economy further deteriorates just the opposite may take place. Interest rates may skyrocket. Once business conditions worsen and bankruptcies mount, the financial world will wake up to realize that "junk bonds" and other types of investments are truly what they are called—JUNK—and very risky. This may cause a real panic in the debt markets as financial institutions, pension funds, foreign investors, etc.

try to unload them. The resultant turmoil could cause interest rates to go through the ceiling and might bring about swift liquidation of some of our overleveraged companies.

Every major depression in our country has snowballed into some kind of panic. The naive and gullible place their trust totally in man's financial institutions and the cherished illusion that prosperity must continue. Eventually, events cause this "trust" to become shattered. The 1930's saw the run on the banks. The 19th century and early parts of this century were also punctuated by numerous financial panics.

In our age, as I have already written, the psychology of insurance has created the grand illusion that everything is under control. Trust in our institutions, in our financial inventions, and in our government is at an all time high. As a result of this trust we have allowed the various financial institutions to squander our nation's money on many high risk investments which will never stand the test of time.

I believe that God is about to shake the financial world and prove again that He, and He alone, is the rock where we can stand. If we put our trust in God first and walk in the Spirit, I believe He will lead us in those areas of sound investment. Furthermore, He will show us again that the soundest investments are "storing treasures in heaven," rather than accumulating riches on earth.

The illusory trust we hold in financial institutions has spread to other financial inventions which have no insurance backing whatsoever. Chief of these inventions is the giant money market funds, which garner over $450 billion. These funds, which pay high interest rates, are like checking and savings accounts to many people. They claim to be as safe as government insured savings accounts because the maturities of their investments are quite short (usually 2-4 weeks). Theoretically, this means a money market fund can retrieve all of its money in about a month. However, this is in theory only. Since these funds invest in companies and concerns which are generally so strapped for funds,they would have a tough time coming up with the money unless they could borrow it from another source. In normal times a company usually can find other sources from which to borrow, if a money market fund does not renew its loan. However, in tough times new sources of credit may be very scarce, and money market funds may prove to be quite illiquid as they are unable to liquidate their loans in a timely manner.

In the coming downturn it just may be that the panic, which historically has been part of "great depressions," may start in the uninsured money market funds. If some of these funds have trouble reimbursing investors, and with media exposure, this could cause a general lack of confidence in all such funds. A "run" on the money market funds could ensue.

Many would say that a run or panic could never happen in our country today. Not too long ago the TV showed long lines of people waiting at banks in Ohio—waiting to secure their savings. This banking chain in Ohio was privately insured, and one of its banks had some financial problems. The newspapers and TV picked up on this problem, and within hours people got scared and ran to the banks to get their money out. The panic was only stemmed when the government stepped in.

What makes our economy so vulnerable to a panic is the very idea that it could never happen here. We have heard the lines over and over again, "your money is safe and sound, not a penny has ever been lost." We have gone fast asleep.

Most people that invest in the money market funds or other types of investments have no idea where their money is going—so great is their trust. If they knew that some of these funds invest in companies that have heavy debt loads and are on shaky ground, they might change their minds. To put it another way, would you take your hard earned savings and invest in a local business without any idea about that business' ability to profit or even survive? I doubt if you would be so foolish.

## A Possible Scenario

Yet, millions of people are trusting their savings to financial experts who, like the false prophets in Jeremiah's day, are saying, "all is well." They can only see unlimited prosperity ahead. It is some of these same experts, who like their counterparts in the Savings and Loan debacle, have invested funds in loans of dubious health and strength.

Are panics possible in modern America? Whether we like it or not the answer is "yes." Anything is possible, including a full scale rout, once that confidence and trust which we have blindly put in financial institutions is abrogated and some of the "junk" investments are revealed. Almost no one believed a crash in the stock market was possible, that is until October 1987. A grain dealer from Kansas had this profound comment to make after the crash, "What people will say, I think, is that day in October 1987 taught a lot of people in our generation that what is here today may be gone tommorrow."[1] Will the government step in to stop any panic? Yes, they will. However, their actions may be more to contain the panic, especially from spreading into the banking system where they have a greater commitment.

The fact that "a panic" is possible in today's economy should jar us out of our sleep. Panics have historically happened with the arrival of great recession/depressions just as stock market crashes are also a part of that history. Secondly, trust or faith in financial institutions, financial experts, and government's abilities to solve economic problems are probably at an all time high. Most people believe that someone else is watching the "store," i.e. someone else has everything under control. This is a prime ingredient for the excessive misuse of funds, as we have already seen in the S&L debacle. Once it is discovered that very few are actually minding the "store," we have the catalyst for a "panic."

In 1876 General George Custer rode on his famous march into the valley of the Little Big Horn. He had only a few hundred troops. Although scouts had told him there were literally thousands of Indians camped in the valley, he rode ahead completely confident of victory. The problem was in Custer's conception of the Indians. He believed, like many other army officers in his day, that Indians would never try to fight the U.S. calvary. Instead, they would flee as fast as they could. It was this erroneous conception which prevented him from taking even basic precautions and, of course, led to his defeat. Today, in our world we still live in an age caught up in half-truths and illusory conceptions. Many, like Custer, believe that financial disaster could not possibly happen in America. Consequently, many basic cautions have been put aside and, like Custer, we too may be totally surprised when ambushed by our "problems."

Jesus said, *you shall know the truth and the truth shall set you free.* As we come to know the truth about ourselves, and about the problems in our society, may God work in us to set us free and to bring that truth to others.

Another area that is likely to suffer in the coming downturn is home equity values. Home ownership in America is probably the only area universally agreed to be a "sure investment." For more than 30 years now the values of homes have increased significantly faster than the inflation rate. This yearly increase in house prices has made many feel significantly wealthier and in turn helped to fuel the borrow and spend spree in our economy. Many have borrowed from their inflated home equities in order to finance the kind of lifestyle suited to them.

Because home ownership has been such a "sure thing" these last few years not only do 75% of families own their own homes, but many speculators and investors have been in the housing market buying and selling. This has been especially true on the West and East coasts where home prices continue to soar every year. Books, investment clubs, partnerships, and TV shows have all devoted considerable time to the idea of achieving wealth through real estate.

Much of the increased inflation in house prices again comes

from "leverage." A home buyer or investor comes in with 5-10% down and finances the rest through credit. It is "easy credit" both to the home buyer and speculator which has helped fuel demand for houses and propelled the prices ever higher.

Unfortunately, there is an adage in the markets that when something becomes a "sure thing," especially in the eyes of the public, the markets will usually behave in a contrary way. Real estate, which has near unanimous approval as an excellent investment, may be on the verge of displaying the contrarian principle. How might this happen? In the case of a severe recession/depression creditors and lending institutions may be extremely damaged by many defaulting loans. As we have shown in earlier chapters, there are already record bankruptcies, defaults and strains on our lending institutions. In the months and years ahead the losses and strains could be enormous. Credit may be much tougher to get, and "easy credit" may become a thing of the past. Without easy credit chasing demand for houses, house sales and ultimately house prices could plummet.

"Leverage" is great for investments, when they are on the rise. If you invest 5% in a house and the house increases say 20% in value, you may double your investment in a very short time. However, "leverage" is bad news when investments are going down in price (as the leverage exerts downward pressure on prices). If real estate prices were to fall for any extended period of time, speculators would bail out in droves, causing more houses to be put on the market and further depressing the prices of houses. What has happened in the farm belt and in places like Alaska, Houston, and Phoenix with falling equity prices could yet be the fate of the rest of America.

In fact, as we get closer to entering the economic downturn, California, the one area of the country having the longest uninterrupted housing boom (22 years), is on the verge of suffering a major breakdown in home prices. In a November

## Like A Bulging Wall

28, 1990 article in the Wall Street Journal entitled *As Home Price Slump Reaches California, Risk to Economy Rises,* Jim Carlton said,

> "The speculative bubble has burst. Since August, demand for new and existing homes in California has plummeted. The value of homes priced above $250,000— a third to half of the market in various parts of the state— has fallen 10-25%. Construction of such homes has practically halted . . . . Dennis Jacobe, chief economist for the U.S. League of Savings Institutions, comments: 'This won't be like the cyclical recessions of the past. **We are so overbuilt that the correction is going to be dramatic.**'
>
> A majority of economists still expect a brief, mild recession. **But some may be underestimating the kind of chain reactions that can be set off by plunges in consumer confidence, home values and construction, especially when many companies and consumers are awash in debt.**"[1]

It just may be that falling real estate prices will be the catalyst which eventually triggers the massive liquidation of debt in our economy. Already in the Northeast, falling real estate prices and defaults have placed tremendous strains on some of the largest New York banks, such as Citicorp and Chase Manhattan. As banks all over the country (especially on the coasts where speculation has been the highest) are forced because of loan problems to cut back on lending, it could in turn create a self-reinforcing credit crunch the likes we have not seen in 60 years. Needless to say, the banking system is going to be a major casualty in the coming downturn in real estate.

Unfortunately for many of us in America, home ownership has become almost idolatrous. Owning one's home has become the dream and hope and pride of one's life. We have worshipped the creation, even our own creations, rather than the Creator. God is going to allow things to be shaken to see if our first love is in Him or in the things we possess. Only in seeking Him and putting our eyes on Jesus will we find the *peace which passes all understanding.*

## Government to Grow

Although God desires all to come to repentance and faith in Him, the coming woes will undoubtedly cause many to turn to the government for answers. A great cry will go up for government to intervene and save the economy. In an article in the Wall Street Journal entitled *Government's Role May Soon Grow Again,* columnist Henry Meyers makes some just arguments for the future growth of government. He states,

> "And the next recession could well be harshest of the postwar lot. Scores of banks and thrift institutions are shaky. Foreign investors could further undercut the U.S. economy if they become frightened and pull out. Many companies are loaded down with high-cost debt in the wake of mergers and leveraged buyouts . . . . Few events short of war tend to concentrate power in Washington as much as do recessions—especially severe recessions."[2]

Alfred Malabre, summarizes a pretty complete scenario of the next economic downturn and also indicates the growth in the role of government. He says,

> "Because of the rigidities and the excesses that now permeate our economy, the next recession will quickly deepen. Business failures will rapidly mount . . . . Unemployment will return to the double digit range. Banks and other thrift institutions will be unable to carry out their financial obligations that will make today's sporatic difficulties seem almost inconsequential. The federal budget deficit will swiftly worsen as revenues diminish; this will complicate government efforts to stimulate a sagging economy. Deflation (falling prices) will be beckioning for sure . . . , but will not take hold as it did during the Great Depression because the **government however reluctantly at first will be stepping in across the entire landscape.**"[3]

## Like A Bulging Wall

It is ironic that problems caused in our economy by trusting in financial institutions and government will probably be handled by increasing government's authority over our lives. Yet this seems again to be the historical pattern. Bigger government was justified in 1932 in order to rescue the country from the Great Depression. During the coming recession, though, the control of government could be substantially greater. Many of our precious freedoms may be restricted. Unfortunately, we will reap that which we have sown. If we as a nation have sown greed and immorality when we had liberty, then we will likely reap a life where that liberty is severely restricted. In fact, for the first time in our history, others, such as the United Nations and Japan, may direct our financial affairs as we attempt to get our house in order. This is the outcome when a country sells itself into slavery.

We will likely find ourselves in a much harsher climate as government grows and seeks to take the steps to solve the crisis. Uncle Sam will undoubtedly unleash the Internal Revenue Service on everyone as it is forced to reduce the deficit. Previous tax breaks that individuals and businesses received may be eliminated. Even the tax exemption for churches and charitable organizations may be reduced or eliminated.

There will be considerable pressure to find scapegoats for the ensuing depression. Rather than face the truth honestly, many will seek to blame others. Free enterprise will be a favorite target of blame and may be used as justification to close or to take over certain businesses. Jews and even evangelical Christians could become targeted as scapegoats.

The coming difficulties will cause a great acceleration towards the cashless money system. Due to the rising loan defaults and credit difficulties, the government will likely have to nationalize the banking system and take over much of the credit card industry. Every transaction may eventually be monitored by the government. Ultimately, debit cards may replace credit cards in our society as transactions get linked directly to bank accounts. Very few will be able to escape the preying eyes of "big brother."

As our country becomes economically weaker, it will be far easier to incorporate it into a one world government. This will not happen overnight, but a sharp recession/depression will surely hasten its advent. We will become one state among a world of many nation states. No longer will our people have a vote on our national affairs, but an international body will govern us. Such is the potential fate of a country living beyond its means by ever accumulating debt.

In the next section we are going to deal with a case scenario. There have been many sections of the country which have played out some of the characteristics of our "possible scenario." There have been places in Texas, New England, Arizona, etc. which have all had some of the characteristics of a collapsing economy. We choose Alaska because as a state it seemed to typify the boom and bust characteristics even more than some of the other areas.

## Case Scenario

Alaska will serve as our case scenario albeit places like Houston and Phoenix have similar problems. Although we are using Alaska's economy to describe some of the potential scenarios for our entire country, it is obvious that Alaska's faltering economy can only reflect some of the possibilities. This is because Alaska is a state and not a nation. It has no Federal Reserve Bank unto itself and cannot deficit spend as our federal governmant does. Therefore, the example we are using will have to be seen in a limited context.

During the 1970's and 1980's Alaska's economy was pumped up by huge oil revenues. It was a boom economy. The oil industry and revenues derived from taxation of this oil provided Alaska with a huge amount of income. Thousands were lured to Alaska as the state embarked on massive public works projects. Highways, bridges, municipal buildings, schools, shopping centers, office buildings, etc. were built during this time. At one point Alaska, with a population of about a half million people, was spending more than the state of California. The sky was the limit as Alaska's economy boomed.

Then the bottom dropped out for Alaska. Starting in 1985, the price of oil fell sharply on world markets, losing more than 60% of its value. When the oil revenues fell, taxation also fell and Alaska was left with just a fraction of its prior income. All over Alaska construction came nearly to a stop, as the state and its economy had to readjust itself to this lower level of income. Thousands lost their jobs and many left Alaska for good. The state was even forced to eliminate 3,500 typically secure jobs of teachers and government workers. As people lost their jobs and some moved away, property values began to plummet. In many cases properties lost 50% of their value in less than 3 years. At one point 12,000 homes and apartments in Anchorage stood vacant or were for sale, while scores of foreclosed and abandoned shopping centers and office buildings dotted the landscape. A number of the commercial and private properties defaulted on their loans, putting severe strain on most of Alaska's banks. Half of Alaska's banks either failed or were merged into stronger banks, and a good share of the remaining banks were put on the "troubled" bank list.

The following is a quote from the Wall Street Journal concerning this plight in Alaska:

> "Anchorage, Alaska—In 1982 Alexandria Sharp and a partner bought an $82,500 condominium in this booming oil and port town. By 1984, the price for identical units in her building had ballooned to $109,000.
>
> 'We thought: This is great. We'll hold on one more year, take our profit and get out,' recalls Ms. Sharp, an Anchorage special-education teacher. But, as Ms. Sharp

and thousands of Alaska homeowners would learn, a year would be too long. In 1985, the state, its economy badly overheated by a spending binge, was rocked by a sudden decline in oil prices. The combination set off an **economic crash** that has ravaged parts of the state's real-estate market, crushed half of its banks, and left its linchpin construction industry battered and struggling for survival. Ms. Sharp, in turn saw the value of her home cut in half . . . . Not long ago, she walked into an Anchorage bank and handed over the keys to her condo, joining a crowd of more than 6,500 Alaskans—virtually one in twelve of the state's mortgage holders—who have lost or surrendered property to foreclosure in the past 12 months."[4]

Although Alaska's economy has recovered a little since this article, there are some parallels we can draw to our national economy. Our national economy, like Alaska's, has been pumped up with an artificial stimulus. Whereas Alaska's economy was pumped up by revenue from oil, our national economy has been pumped up by trillions of dollars of borrowed money. This money, as in Alaska, has served to stimulate the economy and has caused a proliferation of personal and private borrowing and spending. It is this spending as a whole which has given us our record years of prosperity.

When the recession/depression comes to our nation (as it is now beginning to do) and much of this economic stimulus from deficit spending is reduced or ended, we may find like Alaska, there is a painful readjustment coming. Much of the overleveraged debt in our society may come crashing down, causing many bankruptcies and much strain in the banking and financial centers. We will likely have many more banking failures. Property values may suffer significantly—as in Alaska. In Alaska they expect it to take 10 years for the state to recover. As we are finally forced to become a nation "living within our means," it may also take us many many years to recover.

# 9

## How Long Will The Economic Downturn Last?

There is considerable disagreement among the experts concerning the length of time the current economic crisis will last. Many still believe that the recession will be mild and last only a couple of quarters (6 months). Others see the downturn as quite severe, but still are unsure of its duration. Ravi Batra believes the depression could last 7 years. He believes that we had the 7 "fat" years in the 1980's; now, we will experience the 7 "lean" years.

I believe there is much evidence for an economic downturn of long duration. A longer time period fits the classic definition of "depression." As we have already discussed, the stock market crash of 1987 seems to be predicting "depression," not "recession." In the last great depression, which started in 1929, it did not hit bottom until 1933 and it lingered on until World War II started in 1941. In that depression, despite the great suffering, our nation was in much better financial shape. Our nation went into the 1930's depression running a budget surplus, and we were the "creditor" nation to the world. Even though there were years of "lean times," our nation was still financially on solid footing.

Consider the situation in our country now. We have not had a budget surplus in nearly 20 years, and we are the chief "debtor" nation in the world. We are currently running deficits of nearly $250 billion, and these deficits will likely explode upward in the coming crisis. The annual increase in interest on the massive debt alone is more than Congress is able to cut in spending. Furthermore, our country has lost some of its competitive edge in the world marketplace as we have imported far more than we have exported these last few years. To be honest, these are all characteristics of the struggling underdeveloped nations and shows the degree to which our nation has slipped. Therefore, in many ways we are not as strong a country economically as our nation was in the 1930's.

Now, many would say that we have come a long way from the 1930's in terms of controlling economic recessions. It is true that we have a much more active central bank (the Federal Reserve) now than we did in the 1930's—and, we do have a lot more insurance and regulations, etc. to control economic contractions. These devices have perhaps helped prior recessions from developing into depressions. However, using these devices has in the long run served to weaken our credit structure, our banking system, the corporate balance sheets and, of course, the government deficits. There are two anti-recessionary weapons which have now been effectively neutralized as the result of these years of credit deterioration and debt buildup. We shall discuss them next for they have a major bearing on why the duration of this economic downturn may last several years.

## Fiscal and Monetary Policy

As we have mentioned, government traditionally has two anti-recession weapons in its arsenal. The first weapon or method is called fiscal policy. **By fiscal policy we mean that** the government uses its spending, especially deficit spending, as a means or stimulus to pop the economy out of an economic contraction. It is kind of like giving a diabetic a shot of glucose when he has lapsed into an insulin coma. Although increased government deficit spending does not work overnight when our economy is in recession, it does serve to revive it after several months. Some of this increased government spending comes in the form of transfer payments, i.e. unemployment benefits, etc. while other increases can come in the form of tax cuts. In the last recession of 1982-83, large tax cuts for both individuals and businesses served to spur the economy towards this longest peace-time expansion.

The other anti-recession weapon which government traditionally uses is called monetary policy. **In this policy government uses the Federal Reserve Bank to lower interest rates and to increase the money supply during a recession.** By lowering interest rates and increasing the money supply, the Federal Reserve enables credit-starved companies to increase their borrowing and to reduce their interest expense costs on current loans. It also helps to stimulate all those industries which are heavily dependent on credit—auto, housing, etc., by increasing new loan demand for their products. In the last recession interest rates were brought down from a prime rate of 21% to below 10%. This, again, had a mighty effect on our economy. Auto sales were greatly spurred and the housing market boomed in the latter part of the 1980's.

The problem with using goverment stimulus to overcome recessions is that credit excesses never get fully worked out of the economy. Credit excesses build up in the economy when a company, individuals or institutions borrow money but do not use it in the best way. For instance, they might expand the company in a direction where it is not very competitive, or they might use this money to open a new business which is very inefficient. This happens all the time when a company uses borrowed money to purchase another firm which it does not know how to operate.

In a free market economy, recessionary pressures build up when credit becomes scarce. The recession then is a natural part of the economy in that it liquidates many of these inefficient business enterprises and restores the credit these businesses were using back to the economy. It's like a person who gets sick from food poisoning. The symptoms are painful, but they do rid the body of any toxins. Recessions, although painful do rid the economy of poor economic choices and help to rejuvenate it.

The problem with government stimulus during recessions is that they step in and administer the stimulus before the economy has totally cleaned out the economic garbage. Many of these credit excesses and poor business choices continue to get credit infusions. The economy then starts to lose its resiliency as it is forced to carry more and more of these high debt, highly leveraged inefficient firms. Like an addict, the economy never gets fully well before a new dose of stimulation is given. Each time this happens the economy needs ever more stimulus to keep it going. It needs ever more increased amounts of credit and deficit spending in order to get back to recovery. Each time this happens, the debt load and the credit excesses continue to pile up . . . until we have the current situation.

The government's weapons of fiscal and monetary stimulation have been used so much in recent years that now as we stand on the brink of a new economic downturn— these weapons have been largely neutralized. They will probably have very little effect in reviving our economy this time.

Fiscal policy has been left in shambles by the tremendous budget deficits. How can you use deficit spending to stimulate the economy when we are already running $250 billion in the red and growing? During this economic downturn, government is not able to cut taxes and increase spending.

## How Long Will The Economic Downturn Last?

It is being forced to raise taxes and limit spending. The last time our country raised taxes in a recession was in the early 1930's. As we now know this served to deepen that economic contraction into the Great Depression.

An Associated Press article entitled *Not all Economists are Howling over Deficit Package* states:

> "President Bush and Congress are about to turn economic wisdom on its head with a plan to raise taxes and slash spending with the nation seemingly on the verge of a recession . . . . 'Under normal conditions, you don't want to be cutting back on government demand at the same time that private demand is dropping in a recession because that gives a double whammy to the economy,' said David Wyss, chief financial economist for DRI-McGraw Hill Inc.
>
> 'But when things are this far out of kilter, the benefits of solving the underlying structural problem outweigh the short-term damage,' he said. The emerging budget deal in Congress would cut spending throughout the government, raise income taxes on the wealthy and increase the federal gasoline tax, **all contrary to the traditional theory that says spending should be increased and taxes cut during slow times in the hope of stimulating the economy.**
>
> Critics of the deal are warning it will **turn George Bush into Herbert Hoover, another Republican president who preached the need for budgetary prudence as a response to an economic downturn.**"[1]

If the first anti-recession weapon of fiscal policy has been neutralized, what about the second—monetary policy. Surely the Federal Reserve can lower interest rates to stimulate those industries needing easier credit. While it is true the central bank can lower interest rates (and rates will likely come down), where are the credit-worthy borrowers? There is so much "debt" which is bad and so many companies which are on the brink of default that there is a real shortage of credit-worthy borrowers. I believe the coming economic contraction will produce such a fallout of defaults and bankruptcies that great restrictions will be placed on future lending and borrowing activities.

Even if the Federal Reserve is able to lower rates, there will be very few customers able to qualify for this easier credit. We see even now credit being restricted in certain areas of the country (especially the Northeast) where the banks have taken huge losses in real estate and commercial loans.

What will happen without fiscal and monetary stimulation to the economy? The economy will likely take a slow (perhaps fast at times) spiral downward. That spiral works like this: as a group of businesses have trouble or go bankrupt they lay off workers (or reduce the wages of their employees). These employees, now having reduced income, do not make as many purchases. These reduced purchases lead to more business problems and bankruptcies, and the cycle is repeated. Unfortunately, this cycle is self-reinforcing until all the excesses are worked out of the system. Only then, when public confidence is restored and there is ample savings, will a new recovery begin. Without government stimulation, this spiral could last for several years, especially considering the excesses which have been built up.

It is a certainty that government will still try to stop the economic slide even though its major weapons have been neutralized. This will likely result in government takeovers of many financial institutions, and also increased government regulations and control of much of the free market system. Unfortunately, government intervention often makes things worse. It will likely prolong the longevity of the downward cycle.

# 10

# What Then Shall We Do?

*Though the fig tree should not blossom, and there be
no fruit vines, though the yield of the olive should fail,
and the fields produce no food, though the flock should
be cut off from the fold and there be no cattle in the
stalls, yet I will exult in the Lord, I will rejoice in the God
of my salvation* (Habakkuk 3:17-18).

This was a powerful and inspired statement from Habakkuk
who was watching for the impending Chaldean invasion and
the destruction of Israel. Only through the power of the Holy
Spirit could one turn from the losses of property and possessions
and rejoice that he is in the hands of God his Savior.

I believe that we, too, are headed for times of hardship
and distress. Jesus taught in many parables that we are to
be a prepared people—watching the signs of the times, and
understanding what is to come upon the earth. We have a
clear call to persist and even grow in faith as we are ever
mindful of His future coming.

*Consider it all joy, my brethren when you encounter
various trials, knowing that the testing of your faith produces*

109

*endurance. And let endurance have its perfect result that you may be perfect and complete, lacking in nothing* (James 1:2-4).

Such an attitude, such joy and steadfastness can only be accomplished through the Holy Spirit and by growing in a deeper relationship with the One who controls all things.

God often uses trials and hardships to purify His people. He uses these difficulties to show the futility of building treasures on earth "where moth and rust do consume." His impending judgment, like all of God's judgments in history, will again reveal the illusory and transitory nature of things in this world and the vain hope of building anything solid on them. We again find out that we are but dust and that our destiny and glory are meant to be heaven bound.

The pain that we experience in the future will be in direct proportion to the degree that our possessions possess us. It will be directly related to the amount of time and trust we have given over to earthly things rather than spiritual things and the doing of God's will. Paul admonishes us,

> *If you have been raised up with Christ, keep seeking the things above, where Christ is seated at the right hand of God. Set your mind on the things above, not on the things that are on earth. For you have died and your life is hidden with Christ in God* (Colossians 3:1-3).

God's judgment is not meant to leave us in pain but to turn our hearts to His Son and place our faith in Him. It is this faith which rests on a foundation which cannot be moved. The psalmist expresses it well in Psalm 46:1-4,7;

> *God is our refuge and strength, a very present help in trouble. Therefore we will not fear, though the earth should change, and though the mountains slip into the heart of the sea; though its waters roar and foam, though the mountains quake at its swelling pride. There is a river whose streams make glad the city of God . . . . God is in the midst of her, she will not be moved; . . . The Lord of hosts is with us; the God of Jacob is our stronghold.*

## What Then Shall We Do?

Our lord desires that despite the mountains of tumult that might come into our life, we would experience that stream of living water flowing in our spirit. This is the most important thing—that we come to know Him and His eternal life in a far deeper way than we've known before, and to ultimately pass that life on to others. God uses disasters and losses to bring us to cry out for the "living water" which He gave in Jesus Christ and which alone can quench thirst. As David cried out,

> *From the end of the earth I call to Thee when my heart is faint; lead me to the rock that is higher than I. For thou has been a refuge for me, a tower of strength against the enemy* (Psalm 61:2-3).

> *Thy loving kindness is better than life* (Psalm 63:3).

If you have never come to the point of knowing Jesus Christ as your Lord and Savior, now is the time. The One who created you and died on the cross for you waits with open arms for you to receive Him. It is only in the "strength of the Lord" that we will be able to endure the coming times. He has a plan for your life, a high calling. It is a calling which transcends the problems of this world and continues on through eternal life.

If you desire to know Jesus as Lord and Savior, you first need to humble yourself and admit that you are a sinner—that you have been master of your own life and have rebelled against the ways of God. Once you have confessed your sins, you need to open your life up to receive him as your Lord and Savior. He will give you a new heart, new desires, and the Holy Spirit. The Holy Spirit will lead you into all truth and enable you to have the "overcoming life," and the "peace that passes all understanding."

It is important for new Christians as well as older Christians to be joined with a deeply committed Christ-centered church. We are meant to be "members of the Body of Christ." It is only in fellowship with other believers that God is fully able to use us.

It is also important that we get into the Word of God, the Bible. It is in His Word and in prayer that God will lead and guide us.

It would be very easy to pander after our human desires and seek some financial gain in the coming distress. Many so-called "investment books" would lead you to believe that even in the midst of great economic woes, you can still make profits. They would lead you to believe that you can even get rich in the coming turmoil, if you would just invest in gold, silver, coins, or bonds, etc. While it is very tempting to think that you could make a "bundle" out of the coming hardships, this only stimulates our human greed which is the root of the problem. I believe very few people will profit in a financial sense from the coming calamities.

David said, *He makes me to lie down in green pastures* (Psalms 23:2). God will allow troubles to come on us in order to cause us to lie in green pastures—where His Spirit can feed us. When we are engulfed in the drive for material things, no matter how subtle, our energies are often caught up in pursuing that which cannot possibly satisfy our soul. I believe God would have us profit from the coming troubles in a spiritual sense, so that we can be brought back to His green pastures and that our spirit would grow in communion with Him. The Apostle Paul said,

> *But whatever things were gain to me, those things I have counted as loss for the sake of Christ. More than that, I count all things to be loss in view of the surpassing value of knowing Christ Jesus my Lord, for whom I have suffered the loss of all things, and count them but rubbish in order that I may gain Christ* (Philemon 3:7-8).

The investment, then, is that God is after "spiritual fruit"— love, joy, peace, patience, kindness, goodness, etc. If there is any profit to be made in the trouble ahead, let us hope that it is in the knowledge of Him and His will for our lives. As we grow in that knowledge of Him and walk in His Spirit, then we have that peace which "passes all understanding and keeps and guards us through all difficulties." As George Voeks, former pastor of East Immanuel Church was so fond of saying, "As long as we have the joy of the Lord and His Spirit in our heart, it doesn't matter where we are at, whether it be without a home, or in a hospital, or in a nursing home, etc. As long as we have life in Him, we have the riches of eternal life with us wherever we go."

## What Then Can We Do?

Certainly we can call our congressmen and write letters to them. We can urge them into some kind of action concerning the terrible budget deficits. Definitely, we must pray for them. Unfortunately, the problems have persisted for so long, and the people in our government have consistently dodged the issues over time, that many would consider a government solution hopeless.

Jane Bryant Quinn had this to say in a newspaper column with the title *Reaganomics Left Economy so Broke it Can't be Fixed:*

> "The U.S. economy is now so broke that it can't be fixed. At least it can't be fixed for any price that Americans will pay voluntarily.
>
> That's no surprise. For a decade, the reigning 'conservative' orthodoxy has been that government doesn't have to be paid for. One could cut taxes, run the spending machine full tilt, damn the deficit and grow rich.
>
> At a program in March at the University of South Florida, former Treasury Secretary Donald Regan declared that there really are no federal budget deficits— that's just how the government keeps its books. And even if deficits do exist, he said, they've been good for us.
>
> In previous decades, the government also ran up deficits, but at least we worried about them. In what may be the most dangerous legacy of Reaganomics, an

entire generation has grown to adulthood—and voter-hood—in the utter certainty that deficits, although endlessly jawed about, don't really matter. And even if they matter, the orthodoxy goes, that's no excuse to raise a person's tax."[1]

One can see how dangerous the situation has gotten when not even the former treasury secretary recognizes that deficits are bad. It is not he alone but millions of others who cannot recognize what is true and what is false. How can there be a cure when such a condition exists? Jane Bryant Quinn writes further:

"Now we've come to the heart of my fear that the economy is so broke it can't be fixed by any budget cuts that Americans will voluntarily accept. The Congress has been battling over program cuts in the general area of \$20 billion—\$4 billion shy of the potential interest payments on the deficit in 1991. **So the cost of the debt may now be climbing faster than federal spending can be reduced.**

Put another way, any money we chop out of government programs—this year and in the future—won't go to reduce the deficit. It will be eaten up by the mounting interest bill on the national debt.

A decade ago, it was possible to imagine a mix of tax increases and spending cuts that would get America's finances back on track reasonably soon. But no more. **Many years of tough adjustment lie ahead.**"[2]

How can Congress ever solve the problem when (1) it does not realize the gravity of the problem, and (2) it cannot get spending cuts to even cover the rising interest costs. It will take a crisis of some magnitude to galvanize Congress and the government into action. At this point the government is still trying to hide the facts and hide its head in the sand. Often our government seems to manipulate the facts and data to hide rather than reveal the truth. A case in point—even as bad as the Savings and Loan crisis, with billions of dollars in bailout, the government was still trying to hide the true cost by putting some of that cost "off budget." The government has hidden many of its expenditures and growing liabilities "off budget" such that the real deficit will never be known. This fear of facing the truth, even hiding the truth, has been pervasive all through the government. Government often acts like the alcoholic who does not want to admit he has a problem. The alcoholic hides his problem in a little brown sack in the wood pile, while the government hides its problems in off-budget expenditures and grand speeches. You do not solve anything until you come face to face with the truth. Like the alcoholic, our government will undoubtedly have to come face to face with the crisis before things really get changed. Alexander Paris states,

> "There is no simple short-term solution to the problems that ail this country, for they are the results of over thirty years of accumulated financial abuse. The basic cause is excessive government spending, and the excessive credit creation that results from both government actions and the climate they foster. Because they have been in effect unchecked for such a long time, the inflation and credit trends now have an internal momentum of their own. **No less than a complete change in the philosophy of government, accompanied by major reforms in both congressional and administrative budget techniques, is required. There have seldom been any reversals of strongly entrenched government philosophies without a crisis.** There is strong doubt whether any elected government would have the will, ability, morality, and fortitude to engage in the long-term, deliberate action to slow credit growth that would be necessary to cure our financial ills without a serious credit liquidation and financial panic."[3]

As I have mentioned earlier, this book is not primarily an investment manual, for I believe God's objective is to develop spiritual riches in His people. Yet there still needs to be some common defensive measures that one should consider concerning financial matters. The next chapter will deal with some of the practical considerations related to your financial matters. Some of the financial points that I discuss are based on the most likely economic scenario happening (which I have already discussed). If this scenario happens to take a different form or only part of the scenario unfolds, it then is obvious that investment choices may need to be different. However, I believe much of the advise I have given is very conservative, and you will not be hurt by it—even if God spares us some of this judgment.

# 11

## Practical Considerations

### Getting Out of Debt

Since this book is about the consequences of "debt" for our nation, our first consideration must be about getting out of our own personal debt. We need to face the truth about debt in our lives, what it does to us and why it is wrong. Bill Gothard in his *Men's Manual on Financial Freedom* has listed some consequences of borrowing which I feel are very instructive.

1. **Borrowing Violates Scripture.**

   The major verse here is *Owe no man anything, but to love one another* ... (Romans 13:8).

2. **It Constitutes A Judgment Of God.**

   God clearly relates borrowing to His judgment upon His people for failing to follow His ways. (Again, much of my book deals with this judgment on America.)

3. **It Produces Bondage To Creditors.**

   *The borrower is servant to the lender* (Proverbs 22:7). God intends for Christians to be free from earthly entanglements in order to serve Him.

117

4. **It Presumes Upon The Future.**

Borrowing is based on the assumption that future conditions will allow us to repay the debt. God warns against such presumption. (It is especially dangerous in light of coming crisis conditions.)

5. **It Gives The Illusion Of Independence.**

Borrowing gives the temporary illusion of independence from authority. It allows final decisions to be made apart from God's provision of funds. It causes an individual to feel that he is his own authority and that he does not need to wait for wise counsel or sufficient funds. (I discussed this false illusion in prior chapters.)

6. **It Evades Self-Examination.**

When God withholds funds, there is a good reason. It is His signal for us to re-evaluate our lives, our plans for the money, and our faith in Him. Borrowing evades these purposes and allows the Christian to continue in his own wisdom and efforts.

7. **It Interferes With God's Provision.**

God wants to demonstrate His supernatural power through the lives of men and women of faith. Only in this way can He contrast the false confidence which people have placed in their own wisdom, abilities, and riches.

8. **It Removes Barriers To Harmful Items.**

There are many things which we think will be beneficial to our lives, but God knows they will be harmful to us. In His mercy and wisdom he may limit our funds so we cannot afford them.

9. **It Devours Resources Through High Interest Payments.**

Most people who borrow money do not comprehend the final price tag of using someone else's money . . . in the final analysis, interest payments constitute a very large part of the total cost of the loan.

## 10. It Promotes Impulse Buying.

God expects Christians to prayerfully consider their decisions regarding the management of the funds which He provides. In contrast to this, the world encourages buyers to make impulsive decisions based on the desires of the moment. Easy access to money lends itself to impulsive purchases which bypass prayerful thought and wise counsel.

## 11. It Weakens Personal Faith.

In reality, a Christian who relies on credit does not feel that he needs to trust God during the most critical time of decision making. He is convinced that, if he can afford the monthly payments, he can buy the item. However, God wants him to discern whether it is His will to buy it.

## 12. It Causes Overspending.

The credit card system is a major way of borrowing for depreciating items. Credit card users tend to buy more than those who pay cash, and they tend to pay more for the items they do buy.

Behind overspending is a basic lack of self-control. When this is conquered by the power of the Holy Spirit, the habit of borrowing money can also be overcome.[1]

From the above examples it is really quite clear that when we go into debt we are not only violating scripture but we are walking according to the flesh and not the spirit. This can lead to bondage and we may ultimately face God's judgment. Therefore, we need to confess our sins and then try to get out of debt as best as possible. This may mean cutting up credit cards, paying down mortgages, selling assets, etc. Whatever it takes, let the Holy Spirit lead you towards getting out of debt. Aim to become a saver rather than a debtor.

It is far better to take some painful measures now and minimize the pain later on. As difficult as it sounds, consider putting yourself and your family on an austerity budget for a few months. Cut out some of the frills: expensive junk food, fast food meals, trips to the movies and beauty shops. Consider it like a fast—only you are fasting from "self-indulgence." I'm sure you will come out healthier, not only financially, but perhaps physically also.

If the average Japanese person can save 15-20% of his income, so can we. Use the extra savings to pay down debt. This will greatly reduce your interest payments, and give you some breathing room. Also put some of that money away for unexpected expenses and potentially lost income in the coming hard years. Furthermore, those savings may also help lift up a struggling brother or sister in the Lord.

The largest source of debt for most Americans is the home mortgage. It would be nice if one could have this debt paid off. However, in most people's cases it is not practically feasible. Accordingly, the best thing to do would be to try and prepay your mortgage a few months ahead of schedule. If the worst happens and you are unable to make the house payments, because of prepayment you will be in a much safer position. If you are not able to prepay, then at least save as much as you can (to help make any payments if such an emergency arises). Whatever you do, do not go deeper into debt on your home, with a home equity loan or such.

## Savings

Getting out of debt and building up and maintaining savings go hand in hand. I would suggest removing your income from financial institutions where there may be panic withdrawals. I believe this would be most money market funds, many types of bonds, and other higher risk investments. I would suggest putting some of your money in bank accounts, especially strong banks. There are a number of healthy and strong banks in

120

most areas of the country and I have listed a fair number in the appendix. These banks have strong balance sheets and would survive an economic crisis much better than the weaker banks. Insurance probably will not save any banks, but it is my belief that the government and Federal Reserve Bank will try foremost to save the banking system. This is still no guarantee that you will save all your money, but if you choose a strong bank your chances are much better.

## Cash Liquidity

It is a good idea to have some small cash reserves set aside in a place where you do not have to go through a financial institution (this would probably be in your place of residence). In this recession/depression some financial institutions may be closed just as the banks were closed in the 1930's. The cash you have put aside may provide food for you and others in this time of distress. I do not believe you should hoard money in your home, however, a month's supply of income might be very appropriate.

## Employment

The job market will likely be greatly altered in the years ahead. Some industries will come crashing down while others will rise to new prominence. As a result of the false prosperity in our economy, there has built up many service industries which cater to this affluence. To say we have excess capacity in the service industries is to understate the fact. These industries run the gamut from retail chains and malls, professional sports, recreation industries, fast food chains, etc. Even the tremendous growth in colleges and universities have been propelled by massive student loans and easy credit. This is the same easy credit which has built such a false economy.

**In normal economic downturns or recessions the manufacturing industry is the hardest hit—as people postpone spending for big ticket items. Traditionally, the**

service industries have fared better during these times, as consumers have continued (albeit reduced) to maintain these services. Unfortunately, during this downturn the service industries will also be dealt a heavy blow. The coming credit contraction and loan defaults will undoubtedly wring out most of the false prosperity in our age. Easy credit will be a thing of the past. Although credit and credit cards will not disappear, they will be extremely restricted. Service will mostly be on a cash (or debit card) basis. If you work in a service industry occupation, consider the potential vulnerability of your industry along with the economic health of your own particular company.

In the present recession/depression people will likely be keeping their vehicles, houses, furniture, and appliances for a much longer period of time. The repair business will boom. If you are at all handy—now is the time to try and pick up some extra skills at some form of repair, be it auto, plumbing, upholstery, cleaning, video, etc. These extra skills will not only save you much money around your home but could open up job or business possibilities for you in the coming difficult years.

Some other employment areas that will likely hold up better in a severe recession are the medical industries, food industries, parmaceutical industries, railroads, utilities, government jobs, education (the one exception is higher education which might suffer from the credit contraction and student loan defaults). These industries are basically classed as recession proof, because demand for the products they produce remains fairly constant in and out of recessions. Any industry that produces products or services that have become necessities in our economy is a good one to work for.

**Whatever you do in the job market to prepare for the uncertainties of a downturn, make sure you pray and seek the Lord's guidance first, and then perhaps consult with several other people that you highly trust (this could perhaps**

be your pastor or elders in your church). Remember, the Bible says the "wise man" has many counselors. If you are currently in a company with a good balance sheet and low debt load, I would not make a change. Even if the company is in a vulnerable service industry, if it is healthy that company will likely survive. If you move to another company and your seniority is low, you may be the first to go in the coming downturn. However, if you are in an extremely weak company and your seniority is low you might try to change to a job in a more recession proof industry (while there is time). This change might be to a government job, utility company, or perhaps with a food company. Again, there is no guarantee even with these industries, especially if you are low in seniority. This is the time to act with the Lord's help in a very prudent and conservative manner. This is not the time (unless the Lord leads) to transfer to a high risk, more glamorous job.

If your spouse is not working and taking care of the family, this is very commendable. However, it might be prudent, if that person has some education or skills—to bone up on those skills, take some refresher course, even possibly return to work on a part-time basis. This could be a very valuable strategy if the major provider loses his job or a part of his income. If the spouse has little education or that education is greatly outdated, it might again be prudent to take some vocational courses and learn some potentially marketable skills.

## What to do With Your Money or Investments

Remove your money from investments where there may be panic withdrawals, and put it in "safe" investments. This is the time to consider your money and investments from a very conservative point of view. Capital preservation is better than gain. In fact it is my contention that there will be very few money-making investments in the years ahead. Conversely, there may be many, many losers. We want to try and preserve the income and investments which you now have.

123

## Like A Bulging Wall

The two most important questions to ask here are, "What is safe?" and "What is liquid?" By liquidity, we mean how easily can we convert that investment into cash at hand. A banking account is very liquid, it can be converted to cash quite easily, while investment in real estate may not be.

There is nothing which is 100% safe except those riches which are kept for us in heaven. There are some investments though which I believe are much safer than others. I believe the safest and most liquid place to put your savings is a very safe and "strong" bank. As we have already discussed, insurance will not save the banking system. Many banks will fail. However, I believe that Congress and the Federal Reserve will work their hardest to maintain the banking system. Without a banking system commerce would come to a screeching halt. Ultimately, the banking system may be nationalized and put under government control. At that time you still will have access to your money, but there will be much greater restrictions on withdrawals, loans, and interest rates.

If you put your money in a "strong" and "healthy" bank you are more likely to keep your savings secure. A strong bank is a bank that has ample capital, ample liquid cash reserves, and is not overextended in third world loans, junk bond loans, or has significant problems in their investment portfolio. We have listed in the appendix a state by state, city by city listing of the healthier banks in the U.S.

**It is also a good idea to diversify your money into several "strong" banks if possible. This is especially important if you have significant funds on deposit.** There have already been congressional discussions on lowering the $100,000 insurance protection per account, and reducing the number of accounts an individual may have. Furthermore, diversifying protects you if one of your banks still has problems.

Now you're probably going to slam this book shut and say, "I can't make any money at the banks with their low interest rates. I can do much better in the money market funds or in the longer term CD's, or in mutual funds, etc. This is the time to forget about the return on your investments and consider solely the safety of these investments. In the worse case investment scenario you might lose a little bit of money on your investments with the lower interest rates. However, if depression truly does develop in our economy, and many investments go under, then you may be very happy that you were able to preserve your savings.

## Money Market Funds

These have become one of the most popular investments for the public and many businesses these last few years. Over $450 billion are invested in these funds. Some of these money market funds are through insured banks and if it is a "strong" and "healthy" bank will still be fairly safe. However, as I stated earlier, most of the money market funds are not insured and are very short term investments. Government insurance (as discussed earlier) is more a psychological phenomena— most insurance funds do not have adequate capital to meet crisis withdrawals. However, money market funds do not even have the psychology of insurance protecting them. The only protection they have is that everyone says they are very "safe," and there hasn't been any widespread problems with their redemptions. In good times, funds of this type with their short term investments can be fairly reliable. In light of the crisis that we are predicting, what happens when one or more funds cannot pay depositors on a timely schedule? What happens if the media gets this information and everyone sees it on the nightly news? There may be an absolute panic as many try to get their money out of these funds. There could be turmoil in these markets for months. I would avoid these funds at all costs.

## Stocks

The general philosophy that comes from brokerage firms and stock brokers these days is this. They say, "You don't invest in stocks for the short term. No matter what happens to the economy, stocks will always be higher in 4-5 years." While this philosophy has generally been true, consider these exceptions. If you had invested in the stock market at its peak in 1972-73, you would have had to wait until 1982-83 until you recovered from your losses. In the Great Depression of the 1930's the stock market lost 90% of its value from 1929 to 1933. It did not recover until after World War II.

In the coming recession/depression I believe the stock market and mutual funds with stock holdings are not the place to have investments. If there are widespread defaults and bankruptcies, many stocks could end up selling for pennies a share. Furthermore, the climate for business profits may be very, very negative for quite a few years. With institutions wielding their computers, we could likely see the Dow Jones Average plunged back below 1000. Stocks are not the most safe and liquid place to have your investments.

## Real Estate

Again, real estate has been one of the foremost money-making investments in America. There are some residences in our country which have gone up 1000% or more in the last 20 years. Real estate seminars and investment firms still proclaim real estate as the "only sure investment." Obviously, they haven't been talking to people in Houston, or Phoenix, or Alaska, where some home prices have dropped rather dramatically.

Real estate in most cases may not be a good investment for several years. The one exception might still be distressed properties which one could get for a very low price, fix up and sell in a matter of weeks. The real problem with real estate as we have already discussed is supply vs. demand.

## Practical Considerations

With potential widespread unemployment, and defaults on properties there may be a tremendous supply of properties on the market. Even now the government is already in the market in a heavy way—selling properties from failed Savings and Loans. Too much supply of real estate on the market will undoubtedly cause prices to fall.

The other part of the equation in real estate is "demand." Easy credit has been the driving force behind the growth in housing and in real estate prices. I believe the present downturn will make "easy credit" a thing of the past. Credit will likely be much more restrictive in the future. Without easy credit, potential homebuyers will have to come up with a much larger downpayment (and perhaps need a larger income) to qualify for home loans. Demand, then, may dry up for real estate. With slack demand and great supply, real estate prices will very likely go down, perhaps significantly.

Therefore, real estate is not an avenue where I would advise you to put your investments. Prices may fall significantly, and even if they don't, you still may have a tough time selling your properties. Wait a few years, and when the dust settles from the current crisis, you may be able to safely and wisely invest in real estate again.

## Gold and Silver

Many people bought gold and silver in the late 1970's and early 1980's when it looked like inflation was going through the roof and the dollar was self-destructing. Gold leaped up to $800 an ounce and silver more than $40 per ounce. However, gold and silver have not been good investments in the 1980's. The only thing you can say about gold and silver is they are still the only source of "real money." They are worth something because of their scarcity. They will always be considered universally as "money." However, our paper money and our coins (which used to be backed by gold and silver) are "money" because our government says they are, not because they have any intrinsic value.

The only value I can see for holding any silver and gold is for the extreme possibility that the dollar may self-destruct in the coming crisis. This could happen if the Federal Reserve decided to inflate the money supply in order to bail out much of the economy, and it could also happen if there was a general lack of confidence in our currency. My feeling is that these events will probably not happen. However, if you do have some investments in gold and silver, I would continue holding them just in case an extreme crisis in our currency does develop. For those who do not own gold or silver, I would suggest you pray about it. If the Lord speaks to your heart concerning having some gold and silver (for a crisis) then by all means buy some. Do not buy gold and silver expecting to make any profit.

## Government and Corporate Bonds

Government bonds have been historically one of the safest and most liquid investments one could own. However, this may change with the current recession/depression. This change could come about because the mushrooming budget deficits and interest payments on this debt could overwhelm the government's ability to borrow more money. It is possible, as Alfred Malabre has suggested, that the government will not only be forced to limit (or put a cap on) their own interest payments but also limit how much of the bonds you may redeem at any given time. Of course, the government will do this in the name of "national survival." Nevertheless, if this does happen, and you own government bonds, you will feel the pinch. It might be far better at this point to own treasury bills of short duration (3 months or 6 months). You will be far more liquid with these bills and can cash out of them easily if need be. Once the smoke of the crisis clears and the government decides what it is going to do about its debt, you may be able to make a better decision with your investments.

## Practical Considerations

If you're going to be in corporate bonds, the best companies are those rated AAA and have a large cash surplus. These would be companies like IBM, GE, Exxon, etc. These companies are going to have the cash to make interest payments even when business falls flat on its face.

## Municipal Bonds and Funds

Municipal bonds and those funds which invest in these bonds have traditionally been seen as "safe investments." This idea, too, may change as more and more municipalities and states have troubles making interest payments in the economic downturn. Already, there have been enough troubles in this market to warrant this October 29, 1990 Barrons article entitled, *Municipal Bonds, the New Junk?* The article makes the point that some municipal bonds are becoming as risky as "junk bonds." The article states,

> "The municipal bond market's growing dependence on individuals bothers some observers. Robert Muller, a managing director of J.P. Morgan Securities contends that many individual investors totally ignore credit and interest risk in buying municipals. In their anxiousness to avoid taxes, 'they forget that muni's are a capital market like any other with plenty of pitfalls.' He adds, 'without diversification of demand, participants tend to be driven by similar emotions and investment timing.' As a result Muller declares, **'the municipal bond market is more vulnerable to runs than ever before.'** "

Therefore, a person should be very careful and do considerable research if he wishes to invest in some form of municipal bonds. The foremost question should be, "How vulnerable is that municipality in a severe economic crisis?"

## Pension Funds

The problem with many pension funds is the same problem that we find with other insured financial institutions—namely, the Savings and Loans and Banks. Who is watching out to see that the funds are being invested in safe and low risk types of investments? How many people know the portfolio of their company's pension fund? My guess is that almost nobody does. The pension funds have been given a green light to invest in whatever they choose, and appropriately, whatever brings the highest return. As I have discussed earlier, a number of the pension funds along with insurance companies have invested in high risk junk bonds. These bonds carry such a risk that even banks are prohibited by law from purchasing them. A good portion of these bonds will default in the years ahead, even if our country does not experience a severe downturn.

Pension funds also have been some of the largest players in the great stock market rally of the 1980's. Pension funds have been able to show some pretty hefty gains, because of the increase in stock prices. There have been a number of articles written showing that many companies have been able to underfund their contributions to the pension funds because of the rise in stock prices. Therefore, if you take away stock prices, i.e. stock prices become depressed, you may find many underfunded pensions. Furthermore, in hard times, some pension fund investments are going to end up in default. There may be some pension funds going under in the crisis. Whether the government will be able to bail them out as it has the S&L's is a moot point. Government is going to be forced between a rock and a hard place—having to choose whom to bail out and for how much.

If you are in a pension fund or retirement plan now, I would suggest doing some investigating. Find out what their investments are and how safe and liquid they are. There are some good pension funds, and if you belong to one you definitely want to stay with it. However, if you are in a retirement plan that is not solid or you are unsure of—try to roll over those investments into a "strong and healthy" bank.

## Practical Considerations

Whatever you do with your investments, first take it to the Lord in prayer. Then consult with some trusted people that you feel have some solid knowledge in these areas. Make sure your spouse is in agreement with any changes you make. Remember a wise person has many counselors, but the Counsel of the Lord must be first.

In closing, I need to stress that the most important preparation for the days ahead is prayer, prayer and more prayer. We need to pray for our world, for our nation, for our government, for our churches, and for our families. We not only need to pray that God might stay His hand of judgment and the distress might somehow be mitigated, but we also need to pray that God's judgment would have its finished work in our lives and the lives of others. That work is to turn us from the shallowness and transitory value of earthly riches and to cause us to put our trust in God's unchanging and eternal grace through Jesus Christ. Here alone is the sure foundation on which to stand.

# Appendix

# Top Rated U.S. Banks and Savings & Loans

The following lists of banks and Savings and Loans are provided by IDC Financial Publishing. This corporation regularly ranks financial institutions with a ranking designed to measure that institution's health and safety. They rank financial institutions from 1—300. Any institution which receives a mark of 165 or better is considered excellent. We have chosen to list only those financial institutions with ratings of 200 or better and having minimum assets of $100 million. Obviously, there are financial institutions with rating just below 200 that would still be good choices, and secondly there are many smaller banks and S&L's which would also have excellent ratings. There are also some excellent credit unions which we have not listed. If your financial institution is not on the list, it does not necessarily mean that institution is bad, but you should do some more research. For a complete listing and analysis you can write or call IDC Financial Publishing, Inc. The address is:

IDC Financial Publishing, Inc.
P.O. Box 140
Hartland, WI 53029
1-800-544-5457
(a complete national listing runs $100)

If you want to check on the health of your particular bank or obtain a list of the blue ribbon banks in your state, write or call VERIBANC, INC.

VERIBANC, Inc.
P.O. Box 2963
Woburn, MA 01888
1-617-245-8370 or 1-800-442-2657
(there will be a charge)

Also, you can check with the libraries in your locality. Some subscribe to a financial rating service which can give you very valid information on the health of your financial institution.

One has to remember that even good financial institutions can have problems and fall from high ratings in a short period of time. Therefore it is wise to continue to investigate your institution on a periodic basis. However, I believe that the list of Banks and Savings and Loans provided are some of the strongest in the country and have the best chance of weathering the coming economic problems.

# Top Rated U.S. Banks

The following abbreviations are used:

| | |
|---|---|
| B&TC | Bank and Trust Company |
| BK | Bank |
| C | County |
| CMRC | Commerce |
| CMRL | Commercial |
| CTY | City |
| FS&LA | Federal Savings and Loan Association |
| FSB | Federal Savings Bank |
| MSB | Mutual Savings Bank |
| NA | National Association |
| NAT | National |
| NAT ASSN | National Association |
| NB | National Bank |
| NB&TC | National Bank and Trust Company |
| S&LA | Savings and Loan Association |
| ST BK | State Bank |
| SVG | Savings |
| SVG BK | Savings Bank |
| SVG INST | Savings Institution |
| T&SB | Trust and Savings Bank |
| TC | Trust Company |
| TR | Trust |

| Name | City | State | IDC Rank | Assets (Mill. $) |
|---|---|---|---|---|
| FIRST NB | Scottsboro | AL | 242 | 133.18 |
| FIRST NB OF JASPER | Jasper | AL | 238 | 330.25 |
| SOUTHTRUST BK OF ETAWAN NA | Gadsden | AL | 236 | 221.90 |
| SOUTHTRUST BK OF DOTHAN | Dothan | AL | 232 | 408.26 |
| FIRST NB OF TALLADEGA | Talladega | AL | 222 | 101.71 |
| FIRST NB OF WETUMPKA | Wetumpka | AL | 221 | 120.78 |
| SOUTHTRUST BK CULLMAN NA | Cullman | AL | 219 | 135.79 |
| FIRST NB ALEXANDER CITY | Alexander City | AL | 216 | 146.18 |
| SOUTHTRUST BK NA | Montgomery | AL | 208 | 287.74 |
| FIRST ALABAMA BK | Montgomery | AL | 208 | 5,227.75 |
| SOUTHTRUST BK OF HUNTS NA | Huntsville | AL | 207 | 352.69 |
| TROY B&TC | Troy | AL | 200 | 105.12 |
| FIRST NB OF ANCHORAGE | Anchorage | AK | 238 | 1,110.80 |
| FIRST SECURITY BK | Searcy | AR | 300 | 138.73 |
| PEOPLES B&TC | Mountain Home | AR | 277 | 151.42 |
| FIRST NB | Searcy | AR | 246 | 163.08 |
| BANK OF BENTONVILLE | Bentonville | AR | 229 | 250.48 |
| ARKANSAS ST BK | Siloam Springs | AR | 227 | 109.56 |
| BENTON ST BK | Benton | AR | 225 | 154.30 |
| FIRST NB OF CONWAY | Conway | AR | 220 | 192.94 |
| FIRST NB OF SPRINGDALE | Springdale | AR | 214 | 256.90 |

|  |  |  | | |
|---|---|---|---|---|
| FIRST NB OF RUSSELLVILLE | Russellville | AR | 210 | 142.04 |
| CITIZENS NB OF HOPE | Hope | AR | 202 | 144.49 |
| FIRST NB | Paragould | AR | 201 | 163.04 |
| WORTHEN B&TC NA | Little Rock | AR | 200 | 619.48 |
| FIRST INTERSTATE BANCARD NA | Simi Valley | CA | 300 | 248.07 |
| CHINO VALLEY BK | Chino | CA | 282 | 495.96 |
| FEATHER RIVER ST BK | Yuba City | CA | 280 | 125.40 |
| BOREL B&TC | San Mateo | CA | 280 | 156.67 |
| PLAZA BK OF COMMERCE | San Jose | CA | 279 | 516.75 |
| MECHANICS NB | Paramont | CA | 278 | 220.12 |
| COAST COMMERCIAL BK | Santa Cruz | CA | 276 | 118.79 |
| EL CAMINO BK | Anaheim | CA | 275 | 127.15 |
| CALIFORNIA ST BK | Covina | CA | 271 | 252.39 |
| PACIFIC HERITAGE BK | Torrance | CA | 270 | 118.74 |
| EL CAPITAN NB | Sonora | CA | 269 | 117.20 |
| FIRST NORTHERN BK OF DIXON | Dixon | CA | 267 | 177.18 |
| COMMERICAL BK OF FREMONT | Fremont | CA | 266 | 107.07 |
| FAR EAST NB | Los Angeles | CA | 264 | 248.06 |
| SILICON VALLEY BK | Santa Clara | CA | 264 | 572.74 |
| US BK OF CALIFORNIA | Eureka | CA | 263 | 171.38 |
| WELLS FARGO BK NA | San Francisco | CA | 262 | 48,645.07 |
| FIRST COMMERCIAL BK | Sacremento | CA | 261 | 354.15 |
| BANK OF MONTECITO | Montecito | CA | 260 | 197.27 |
| COUNTY BK OF MERCED | Merced | CA | 257 | 129.99 |

*Continued*

137

# Like A Bulging Wall

| Name | City | State | IDC Rank | Assets (Mill. $) |
|---|---|---|---|---|
| REDDING BK OF COMMERCE | Redding | CA | 255 | 101.92 |
| FINANCIAL CENTER BK NA | San Francisco | CA | 254 | 280.87 |
| SANTA MONICA BK | Santa Monica | CA | 254 | 807.47 |
| MID-STATE BK | Arroyo Grande | CA | 252 | 714.24 |
| SOUTH VALLEY NB | Morgan Hill | CA | 252 | 122.01 |
| SANTA BARBARA B&TC | Santa Barbara | CA | 251 | 764.45 |
| GENERAL BK | Los Angeles | CA | 250 | 731.94 |
| EXCHANGE BK | Santa Rosa | CA | 249 | 539.36 |
| MODESTO BKG CO | Modesto | CA | 247 | 170.26 |
| FARMERS & MERCHANTS BK OF LONG BEACH | Long Beach | CA | 246 | 1,284.01 |
| HOME BK | Signal Hill | CA | 246 | 379.34 |
| FIRST AMERICAN BK | Rosemead | CA | 245 | 168.19 |
| HANMI BK | Los Angeles | CA | 245 | 230.88 |
| NATIONAL BK OF SOUTHERN CALIFORNIA | Santa Ana | CA | 244 | 313.26 |
| KYOWA BK OF CALIFORNIA | Los Angeles | CA | 242 | 102.10 |
| CATHAY BK | Los Angeles | CA | 242 | 615.80 |
| SANTA CLARITA NB | Valencia | CA | 242 | 254.07 |
| GROSSMONT BK | La Mesa | CA | 242 | 338.07 |
| SAVINGS BK OF MENDOCINO CITY | Ukiah | CA | 241 | 267.27 |
| BANK OF WALNUT CREEK | Walnut Creek | CA | 241 | 115.83 |
| AMERICAN VALLEY BK | El Cajon | CA | 241 | 113.20 |
| GUARDIAN BK | Los Angeles | CA | 240 | 459.38 |

138

## Top Rated U.S. Banks

| | | | |
|---|---|---|---|
| RIVERSIDE NB | Riverside | CA | 240 | 254.14 |
| FIRST NB OF MONTEREY CITY | Monterey | CA | 239 | 184.18 |
| BANK OF NEWPORT | Newport Beach | CA | 238 | 276.91 |
| PACIFIC WESTERN BK | San Jose | CA | 236 | 1,288.14 |
| CALIFORNIA CENTER BK | Los Angeles | CA | 236 | 137.32 |
| ASSOCIATES NB | Pleasanton | CA | 235 | 128.70 |
| BANK OF HEMET | Hemet | CA | 232 | 104.22 |
| MARATHON NB | Los Angeles | CA | 232 | 148.76 |
| TRUCKEE RIVER BK | Truckee | CA | 231 | 142.24 |
| NORTH COUNTY BK | Escondido | CA | 229 | 161.40 |
| ELDORADO BK | Tustin | CA | 228 | 291.14 |
| FIRST CHARTER BK NA | Beverly Hills | CA | 227 | 179.89 |
| CALIFORNIA REPUBLIC BK | Bakersfield | CA | 227 | 539.82 |
| CITY NB | Beverly Hills | CA | 227 | 4,884.95 |
| FIRST NB | Daly City | CA | 226 | 170.84 |
| BANK OF INDUSTRY | City of Industry | CA | 226 | 224.58 |
| BANK OF SANTA CLARA | Santa Clara | CA | 225 | 141.25 |
| PACIFIC VALLEY NB | Modesto | CA | 224 | 114.22 |
| BANK OF THE SIERRA | Porterville | CA | 220 | 118.62 |
| WESTERN BK | Los Angeles | CA | 220 | 293.00 |
| COMMERCIAL CENTER BK | Santa Ana | CA | 220 | 248.00 |
| TRANS-WORLD BK | Sherman Oaks | CA | 220 | 219.05 |
| FIRST VALLEY BK | Lompoc | CA | 219 | 100.60 |
| LINCOLN NB | Encino | CA | 218 | 532.57 |

*Continued*

139

# Like A Bulging Wall

| Name | City | State | IDC Rank | Assets (Mill. $) |
|------|------|-------|----------|------------------|
| FOOTHILL INDEPENDENT BK | Glendora | CA | 218 | 239.34 |
| PIONEER BK | Fullerton | CA | 218 | 189.32 |
| UNIVERSITY NB&TC | Palo Alto | CA | 217 | 277.83 |
| PACIFIC BK NA | San Francisco | CA | 215 | 785.64 |
| FARMERS & MERCHANTS BK OF CALIFORNIA | Lodi | CA | 215 | 497.30 |
| MISSION VIEJO NB | Mission Viejo | CA | 214 | 153.36 |
| FIRST BUSINESS BK | Los Angeles | CA | 214 | 522.79 |
| CUPERTINO NB | Cupertino | CA | 214 | 118.17 |
| BANK OF A LEVY | Ventura | CA | 213 | 614.36 |
| ANTELOPE VALLEY BK | Lancaster | CA | 213 | 139.51 |
| AMERICAN INTL BK | Los Angeles | CA | 213 | 341.51 |
| BANK OF SANTA MARIA | Santa Maria | CA | 211 | 168.07 |
| AMERICAN COMMERCE NB | Anaheim | CA | 211 | 127.34 |
| FIRST ST BK OF THE OAKS | Thousand Oaks | CA | 210 | 154.42 |
| BANK OF SALINAS | Salinas | CA | 210 | 145.01 |
| ALAMEDA FIRST NB | Alameda | CA | 209 | 213.58 |
| IMPERIAL BK | Inglewood | CA | 208 | 2,887.47 |
| BANK OF STOCKTON | Stockton | CA | 208 | 671.66 |
| SECURITY PACIFIC ST BK | Irvine | CA | 207 | 308.33 |
| STERLING BK | Los Angeles | CA | 207 | 145.15 |
| AMERICAN PACIFIC ST BK | N. Hollywood | CA | 207 | 197.21 |
| SOUTH BAY BK | Torrance | CA | 206 | 120.20 |

140

# Top Rated U.S. Banks

|  |  |  | | |
|---|---|---|---|---|
| NORTH VALLEY BK | Redding | CA | 205 | 132.85 |
| BANK OF SAN PEDRO | Los Angeles | CA | 204 | 183.59 |
| MECHANICS BK OF RICHMOND | Richmond | CA | 204 | 604.08 |
| SACRAMENTO COMMERCIAL BK | Sacramento | CA | 204 | 114.13 |
| LA JOLLA B&TC | La Jolla | CA | 203 | 516.46 |
| TOKAI BK OF CALIFORNIA | Los Angeles | CA | 202 | 1,196.87 |
| RANCHO SANTA FE NB | Rancho Santa Fe | CA | 200 | 148.55 |
| FIRST NB IN LOVELAND | Loveland | CO | 247 | 125.92 |
| LAKESIDE NB | Wheat Ridge | CO | 237 | 137.08 |
| UNITED BK OF MONTROSE NA | Montrose | CO | 233 | 125.09 |
| FIRST NB IN BOULDER | Boulder | CO | 214 | 333.12 |
| MOUNTAIN STATES BK | Denver | CO | 205 | 149.29 |
| SEYMOUR TC | Seymour | CT | 289 | 129.33 |
| GREENWOOD TC | Newcastle | DE | 300 | 5,499.68 |
| MIDATLANTIC NB DELAWARE | Wilmington | DE | 300 | 312.70 |
| BENEFICIAL NB | Wilmington | DE | 300 | 244.34 |
| SOVRAN BK DELAWARE | Dover | DE | 300 | 135.93 |
| CHASE MANHATTAN BK (USA) | Wilmington | DE | 294 | 9,606.21 |
| FCC NB | Wilmington | DE | 290 | 4,236.26 |
| FIRST ATLANTA BK NA | New Castle | DE | 282 | 144.74 |
| BANK OF NEW YORK-DELAWARE | Wilmington | DE | 279 | 4,532.92 |
| BOATMENS BK OF DELAWARE | New Castle | DE | 279 | 239.15 |

Continued

| Name | City | State | IDC Rank | Assets (Mill. $) |
|---|---|---|---|---|
| CORESTATES BK OF DELAWARE NA | Wilmington | DE | 274 | 828.65 |
| MELLON BK DELAWARE NA | Wilmington | DE | 274 | 1,158.06 |
| WILMINGTON TC | Wilmington | DE | 270 | 3,622.40 |
| J.C.PENNEY NB | Harrington | DE | 266 | 568.50 |
| FIRST OMNI BK NA | Millsboro | DE | 264 | 596.68 |
| PRIMERICA BK | Newark | DE | 263 | 372.94 |
| AMERICAN EXPRESS CENTRION BK | Newark | DE | 262 | 9,136.75 |
| MORGAN BK DELAWARE | Wilmington | DE | 252 | 4,881.77 |
| NBD DELAWARE BK | Newark | DE | 246 | 305.86 |
| BANKERS TR DELAWARE | Wilmington | DE | 236 | 2,713.17 |
| PNC NB | Wilmington | DE | 229 | 701.09 |
| FIRST USA BK | Wilmington | DE | 228 | 1,490.41 |
| COLONIAL NB USA | Wilmington | DE | 219 | 1,208.99 |
| DELAWARE TC | Wilmington | DE | 213 | 1,404.83 |
| BALTIMORE TC | Selbyville | DE | 211 | 202.40 |
| UNITED MISSOURI BK USA | New Castle | DE | 208 | 126.39 |
| MANUFACTURERS HANOVER BK | Wilmington | DE | 203 | 1,723.00 |
| SOVRAN BK DC NAT | Washington | DC | 239 | 1,000.77 |
| CITIZENS BK WASHINGTON NA | Washington | DC | 218 | 180.96 |
| BARNETT BK TC NA | Jacksonville | FL | 300 | 108.15 |
| WAUCHULA ST BK | Wauchula | FL | 288 | 156.42 |

142

# Top Rated U.S. Banks

|  |  |  | |  |
|---|---|---|---|---|
| SUNSHINE BK | Pensacola | FL | 269 | 134.63 |
| NORTHERN TR BK OF FLORIDA NA | Sarasota | FL | 268 | 149.45 |
| NORTHERN TR BK OF FLORIDA NA | Naples | FL | 266 | 122.27 |
| UNITED NB | Miami | FL | 265 | 426.54 |
| BEACH BK OF VERO BEACH | Vero Beach | FL | 265 | 163.23 |
| NORTHERN TR BK OF FLORIDA NA | Miami | FL | 262 | 572.40 |
| BARNETT BK SAINT JOHNS | St. Augustine | FL | 261 | 395.53 |
| BARNETT BK OF NAPLES | Naples | FL | 255 | 707.03 |
| HILLSBORO SUN BK | Plant City | FL | 255 | 192.56 |
| SUN BK TREASURE COAST NA | Vero Beach | FL | 247 | 562.94 |
| BARNETT BK OF JACKSONVILLE NA | Jacksonville | FL | 246 | 1,967.62 |
| BARNETT BK OF LEE CITY NA | Fort Myers | FL | 242 | 759.39 |
| BARNETT BK OF THE KEYS | Key West | FL | 241 | 420.97 |
| RIVERSIDE NB OF FLORIDA | Fort Pierce | FL | 239 | 171.51 |
| CITIZENS BK | Marianna | FL | 237 | 112.16 |
| SUN B&TC | Brooksville | FL | 234 | 544.41 |
| BARNETT BK OF LAKE CITY NA | Eustis | FL | 234 | 386.47 |
| SUN BK OF VOLUSIA CITY | Daytona Beach | FL | 233 | 641.52 |
| SUN B&TC CHARLOTTE CITY NA | Port Charlotte | FL | 233 | 334.53 |
| BARNETT BK OF LAKE OKEECHOBEE | Okeechobee | FL | 232 | 182.80 |
| ORANGE BK | Ocoee | FL | 229 | 232.68 |
| TIB BK KEYS | Key Largo | FL | 228 | 157.00 |
| SUN BK LEE COUNTY NA | Fort Myers | FL | 228 | 510.50 |
| SUN BK TALLAHASSEE NA | Tallahassee | FL | 227 | 167.33 |

*Continued*

143

| Name | City | State | IDC Rank | Assets (Mill. $) |
|---|---|---|---|---|
| BARNETT BK OF CENTRAL FLORIDA NA | Orlando | FL | 225 | 2,590.27 |
| FIRST GUARANTY B&TC | Jacksonville | FL | 224 | 102.24 |
| CITIZENS NB | Naples | FL | 223 | 171.29 |
| SUN FIRST NB OF POLK COUNTY | Winter Haven | FL | 222 | 512.51 |
| KEY BISCAYNE B&TC | Key Biscayne | FL | 221 | 105.13 |
| BARNETT BK OF NORTH CENTRAL FLORIDA | Lake City | FL | 219 | 254.76 |
| SUN BK NAPLES NA | Naples | FL | 218 | 263.04 |
| SUN COMMERCIAL BK | Panama City | FL | 218 | 221.62 |
| BARNETT BK OF HIGHLANDS CITY | Sebring | FL | 216 | 412.69 |
| FIRST NB | Venice | FL | 215 | 368.88 |
| FIRST NB OF SANTA ROSA | Milton | FL | 215 | 127.13 |
| KISLAK NB | North Miami | FL | 214 | 224.22 |
| COCONUT GROVE BK | Miami | FL | 213 | 209.08 |
| COMMUNITY BK OF HOMESTEAD | Dade County | FL | 213 | 167.41 |
| BARNETT BK OF VOLUSIA CITY | DeLand | FL | 212 | 961.17 |
| BARNETT BK OF TALLAHASSEE | Tallahassee | FL | 210 | 485.26 |
| BARNETT BK OF MARION COUNTY NA | Ocala | FL | 210 | 489.39 |
| TRANSFLORIDA BK | Cooper City | FL | 208 | 118.90 |
| CITIZENS NB OF LEESBURG | Leesburg | FL | 204 | 278.03 |
| BARNETT BK OF MANATEE C NA | Bradenton | FL | 201 | 717.72 |
| COLUMBUS BK COMPANY | Columbus | GA | 289 | 992.39 |
| TRUST CO BK OF MIDDLE GEORGIA NA | Macon | GA | 286 | 485.37 |

# Top Rated U.S. Banks

| Bank | City | State | Rank | Value |
|---|---|---|---|---|
| GRANITE CITY BK | Elberton | GA | 282 | 110.41 |
| COMMERCIAL BK | Thomasville | GA | 280 | 165.28 |
| TRUST CO BK | Atlanta | GA | 278 | 5,969.46 |
| TRUST CO BK SAVANNAH NA | Savannah | GA | 277 | 386.97 |
| TRUST CO BK OF ROCKDALE | Conyers | GA | 276 | 199.21 |
| MONOGRAM CREDIT CARD BK | Roswell | GA | 265 | 945.33 |
| BANK SOUTH MACON | Macon | GA | 264 | 365.75 |
| BANK OF THOMSON | Thomson | GA | 263 | 105.43 |
| TRUST CO BK GWINNETT CITY | Lawrenceville | GA | 256 | 247.38 |
| FARMERS & MERCHANTS BK | Summerville | GA | 255 | 103.56 |
| FIRST NB OF GAINESVILLE | Gainesville | GA | 255 | 814.58 |
| TRUST CO BK OF NORTHEAST GEORGIA | Athens | GA | 252 | 312.13 |
| FARMERS & MERCHANTS BK | Dublin | GA | 250 | 137.41 |
| BANK OF CLAYTON | Clayton | GA | 248 | 123.04 |
| FIRST ST BK | Stockbridge | GA | 247 | 113.17 |
| TRUST CO BK OF COFFEE CITY | Douglas | GA | 247 | 104.15 |
| FIRST NB OF HABERSHAM | Cornelia | GA | 242 | 111.88 |
| TRUST CO BK OF SOUTHEAST GEORGIA NA | Brunswick | GA | 239 | 319.78 |
| TRUST CO BK-AUGUSTA NA | Augusta | GA | 237 | 328.72 |
| SOUTHEASTERN BK | Folkston | GA | 230 | 119.21 |
| BANK OF COVINGTON | Covington | GA | 230 | 116.60 |
| BANK OF DAHLONEGA | Dahlonega | GA | 230 | 116.96 |
| BRAND BANKING COMPANY | Lawrenceville | GA | 226 | 171.13 |
| TRUST CO BK OF NORTHWEST GEORGIA NA | Rome | GA | 222 | 234.42 |

*Continued*

145

# Like A Bulging Wall

| Name | City | State | IDC Rank | Assets (Mill. $) |
|------|------|-------|----------|------------------|
| FIRST BULLOCH B&TC | Statesboro | GA | 220 | 143.31 |
| MOULTRIE NB | Moultrie | GA | 220 | 117.26 |
| BANK OF CANTON | Canton | GA | 219 | 159.22 |
| SECURITY B&TC | Albany | GA | 219 | 115.22 |
| FIRST NB IN ELBERTON | Elberton | GA | 217 | 109.99 |
| TRUST COMPANY BK COLUMBUS NA | Columbus | GA | 216 | 254.72 |
| NORTHWEST GEORGIA BK | Ringgold | GA | 216 | 107.85 |
| BANK SOUTH OF WAYCROSS | Waycross | GA | 213 | 168.65 |
| BANK OF COWETA | Newnan | GA | 210 | 118.31 |
| UNION COUNTY BK | Blairsville | GA | 209 | 127.11 |
| FIRST NB OF GRIFFIN | Griffin | GA | 207 | 136.72 |
| TRUST COMPANY BK OF CLAYTON CITY | Jonesboro | GA | 207 | 130.72 |
| SEA ISLAND BK | Statesboro | GA | 201 | 130.37 |
| CITY BK | Honolulu | HI | 280 | 598.72 |
| GECC FINANCIAL CORP | Honolulu | HI | 275 | 595.46 |
| FIRST HAWAIIAN CREDITCP INC | Honolulu | HI | 248 | 321.35 |
| FIRST HAWAIIAN BK | Honolulu | HI | 234 | 5,171.84 |
| BANK OF HAWAII | Honolulu | HI | 232 | 8,662.14 |
| FIRST INTERSTATE BK HAWAII | Honolulu | HI | 229 | 858.24 |
| CENTRAL PACIFIC BK | Honolulu | HI | 221 | 950.26 |
| FINANCE FACTORS | Honolulu | HI | 216 | 230.01 |

# Top Rated U.S. Banks

| | | | | |
|---|---|---|---|---|
| KEY BK IDAHO | Boise | ID | 289 | 682.27 |
| BANK OF COMMERCE | Idaho Falls | ID | 217 | 176.78 |
| FIRST INTERSTATE BK IDAHO NA | Boise | ID | 215 | 903.31 |
| FIRST ST B&TC | Park Ridge | IL | 300 | 162.81 |
| LINCOLN NB | Chicago | IL | 300 | 366.44 |
| RIVER FOREST STATE B&TC | River Forest | IL | 293 | 266.12 |
| FIRST NB OF CICERO | Cicero | IL | 286 | 216.39 |
| NBD ELK GROVE BK | Elk Grove Village | IL | 283 | 310.80 |
| HARRIS BK WINNETKA NA | Winnetka | IL | 280 | 227.91 |
| COMMERCIAL NB OF CHICAGO | Chicago | IL | 275 | 292.53 |
| DIXON NB | Dixon | IL | 265 | 236.97 |
| HARRIS BK GLENCOE-NORTHBROOK NA | Glencoe | IL | 264 | 215.84 |
| FIRST NB IN HARVEY | Harvey | IL | 262 | 113.23 |
| FIRST NB OF LA GRANGE | La Grange | IL | 261 | 109.24 |
| WEST SUBURBAN BK | Lombard | IL | 260 | 326.23 |
| SUBURBAN BK OF BARRINGTON | Barrington | IL | 253 | 101.80 |
| FIRST AMERICAN BK | Dundee | IL | 253 | 117.32 |
| WEST SUBURBAN BK CARROL STREAM | Bloomingdale | IL | 252 | 135.33 |
| HERITAGE BK TINLEY PARK | Tinley Park | IL | 251 | 212.56 |
| GARY-WHEATON BK NA | Wheaton | IL | 251 | 843.98 |
| HOME STATE BK NA | Crystal Lake | IL | 251 | 178.49 |
| STATE BK OF COUNTRYSIDE | Countryside | IL | 251 | 164.67 |
| BANK OF O'FALLON | O'Fallon | IL | 249 | 150.58 |
| LARKIN BK | Hoofman Estates | IL | 249 | 114.59 |

*Continued*

147

| Name | City | State | IDC Rank | Assets (Mill. $) |
|---|---|---|---|---|
| COUNTRYSIDE BK | Mount Prospect | IL | 247 | 120.60 |
| FIRST ILLINOIS BK EVANSTON NA | Evanston | IL | 246 | 693.51 |
| NBD HIGHLAND PARK NA | Highland Park | IL | 245 | 435.80 |
| FIRST BK ILLINOIS | O'Fallon | IL | 244 | 236.29 |
| BOATMENS NB CHARLESTON | Charleston | IL | 244 | 118.45 |
| LASALLE BK LISLE | Lisle | IL | 244 | 148.05 |
| FIRST ILLINOIS BK OF WILMETTE | Wilmette | IL | 244 | 347.52 |
| ALTON MERCANTILE BK NA | Alton | IL | 243 | 226.82 |
| GARY-WHEATON BK BATAVIA NA | Batavia | IL | 240 | 150.93 |
| STANDARD B&TC | Hickory Hills | IL | 239 | 117.99 |
| FIRST SECURITY T&SB | Elmwood Park | IL | 239 | 209.61 |
| ELLIOTT ST BK | Jacksonville | IL | 238 | 170.88 |
| LASALLE NW NB | Chicago | IL | 238 | 822.74 |
| HERITAGE BK&TC | Blue Island | IL | 238 | 230.89 |
| NBD SKOKIE BK NA | Skokie | IL | 238 | 434.06 |
| NBD ARLINGTON HEIGHTS BK | Arlington Heights | IL | 237 | 245.08 |
| BANK OF BUFFALO GROVE | Buffalo Grove | IL | 235 | 109.12 |
| COLONIAL BK | Chicago | IL | 235 | 344.98 |
| MCHENRY ST BK | McHenry | IL | 234 | 341.07 |
| BANK OF WAUKEGAN | Waukegan | IL | 233 | 268.95 |
| BLACKHAWK ST BK | Milan | IL | 233 | 112.12 |
| MAYWOOD PROVISO ST BK | Maywood | IL | 233 | 107.41 |

# Top Rated U.S. Banks

|  |  |  | | |
|---|---|---|---|---|
| FIRST NB | Mount Prospect | IL | 232 | 361.46 |
| BANK OF ALTON | Alton | IL | 232 | 123.89 |
| FIRST AMERICAN BK | Skokie | IL | 232 | 180.29 |
| EXCHANGE BK RIVER OAKS | Calumet City | IL | 231 | 202.24 |
| STATE BK OF ANTIOCH | Antioch | IL | 231 | 185.39 |
| NBD PARK RIDGE BK | Park Ridge | IL | 231 | 599.01 |
| WEST SUBURBAN BK OF DARIEN | Darien | IL | 230 | 164.28 |
| BANK CHICAGO-GARFIELD RIDGE | Chicago | IL | 229 | 110.73 |
| FIRST NB OF LAKE ZURICH | Lake Zurich | IL | 229 | 102.78 |
| FIRST NB OF ILLINOIS | Lansing | IL | 228 | 183.76 |
| AMERICAN NB MELROSE PARK | Melrose Park | IL | 226 | 131.35 |
| LA SALLE NB | Chicago | IL | 226 | 1,391.74 |
| HARRIS BK NA | Barrington | IL | 225 | 426.66 |
| SOUTH HOLLAND T&SB | South Holland | IL | 224 | 359.70 |
| FIRST T&SB | Taylorville | IL | 223 | 151.32 |
| NATIONAL BK OF MENDOTA | Mendota | IL | 222 | 106.68 |
| NEW LENOX ST BK | New Lenox | IL | 222 | 220.06 |
| BANK OF LINCOLNWOOD | Lincolnwood | IL | 222 | 235.78 |
| ITASCA B&TC | Itasca | IL | 221 | 157.30 |
| FIRST MIDWEST BK/WESTERN NA | Moline | IL | 221 | 270.21 |
| MID CITY NB OF CHICAGO | Chicago | IL | 219 | 347.79 |
| OAK LAWN NB | Oak Lawn | IL | 218 | 272.76 |
| AMERICAN NB&TC OF WAUKEGAN | Waukegan | IL | 218 | 177.56 |
| CHICAGO CITY B&TC | Chicago | IL | 218 | 197.05 |

*Continued*

| Name | City | State | IDC Rank | Assets (Mill. $) |
|---|---|---|---|---|
| NBD NORTHFIELD BK | Northfield | IL | 217 | 114.09 |
| OLD SECOND NB | Aurora | IL | 217 | 297.93 |
| UNITED ILLINOIS BK | Benton | IL | 216 | 138.96 |
| WEST SUBURBAN BK DOWNERS GROVE | Downers Grove | IL | 216 | 125.83 |
| LAKE SHORE NB | Chicago | IL | 216 | 818.71 |
| LA SALLE BK WESTMONT | Westmont | IL | 215 | 152.47 |
| BANK OF HOMEWOOD | Homewood | IL | 215 | 140.27 |
| COLUMBIA NB OF CHICAGO | Chicago | IL | 214 | 453.94 |
| MANUFACTURERS BK | Chicago | IL | 214 | 330.62 |
| HARRIS BK ARGO | Summit | IL | 214 | 107.31 |
| PARK NB OF CHICAGO | Chicago | IL | 212 | 178.20 |
| FIRST NB OF ELGIN | Elgin | IL | 212 | 468.23 |
| GLENVIEW ST BK | Glenview | IL | 211 | 410.80 |
| SOY CAPITAL B&TC | Decatur | IL | 211 | 104.22 |
| FIRST MIDWEST BK NA | Waukegan | IL | 210 | 831.79 |
| MID TOWN B&TC | Chicago | IL | 209 | 121.44 |
| HARRIS BK ST CHARLES | St. Charles | IL | 209 | 203.37 |
| LA SALLE BK LAKE VIEW | Chicago | IL | 209 | 600.91 |
| BANK OF MARION | Marion | IL | 209 | 119.79 |
| BANK OF HERRIN | Herrin | IL | 208 | 101.12 |
| STANDARD B&TC | Evergreen Park | IL | 208 | 261.19 |
| AMERICAN NB OF ARLNGTON HEIGHTS | Arlington Heights | IL | 206 | 149.04 |

# Top Rated U.S. Banks

| | | | |
|---|---|---|---|
| BANK OF HIGHLAND PARK | Highland Park | IL | 206 | 217.02 |
| SOUTH SIDE T&SB | Peoria | IL | 206 | 144.38 |
| PARKWAY B&TC | Harwood Heights | IL | 206 | 332.19 |
| BANK OF EDWARDSVILLE | Edwardsville | IL | 205 | 278.47 |
| CLEARING BK | Chicago | IL | 205 | 131.56 |
| INDEPENDENCE BK OF CHICAGO | Chicago | IL | 205 | 136.61 |
| FIRST NB OF NILES ILINOIS | Niles | IL | 205 | 205.34 |
| FIRST OF ILLINOIS B&T | La Grange | IL | 204 | 457.52 |
| NORTHERN TR BK/LAKE FOREST NA | Lake Forest | IL | 204 | 551.11 |
| NBD EVANSTON BK NA | Evanston | IL | 203 | 582.53 |
| FIRST NB OF JOLIET | Joliet | IL | 203 | 401.43 |
| HARRIS BK HINSDALE NA | Hinsdale | IL | 202 | 385.28 |
| FIRST NB OF DANVILLE | Danville | IL | 201 | 143.57 |
| MARQUETTE NB | Chicago | IL | 201 | 502.12 |
| NATIONAL BK OF CANTON | Canton | IL | 201 | 130.12 |
| AFFILIATED BK WESTERN NAT | Cicero | IL | 201 | 220.19 |
| FIRST NB IN DE KALB | De Kalb | IL | 201 | 128.48 |
| AFFILIATED BK | Franklin Park | IL | 200 | 266.02 |
| AMERICAN NB&TC OF MUNCIE | Muncie | IN | 250 | 189.42 |
| BANK ONE NA | Bloomington | IN | 245 | 322.46 |
| MID STATE BK OF HENDRICKS CITY | Danville | IN | 236 | 125.28 |
| PEOPLES B&TC | Mt. Vernon | IN | 236 | 119.54 |
| BANK ONE | Plainfield | IN | 235 | 147.83 |
| BANK ONE CRAWFORDSVILLE NA | Crawfordsville | IN | 229 | 139.71 |

*Continued*

151

| Name | City | State | IDC Rank | Assets (Mill. $) |
|------|------|-------|----------|------------------|
| FIFTH THIRD BK SOUTHEASTERN | Greensburg | IN | 228 | 201.78 |
| FIRST NB | Kokomo | IN | 224 | 227.83 |
| BANK ONE MERRILLVILLE NA | Gary | IN | 216 | 501.51 |
| FIRST BK OF BERNE | Berne | IN | 215 | 163.36 |
| INDIANA ST BK | Terre Haute | IN | 215 | 102.35 |
| CITIZENS NB OF TELL CITY | Tell City | IN | 214 | 128.93 |
| SUMMIT BK | Marion | IN | 211 | 163.92 |
| MID STATE BK | Zionsville | IN | 210 | 103.37 |
| FIRST NB OF WARSAW | Warsaw | IN | 208 | 290.36 |
| CALUMET NB | Hammond | IN | 207 | 430.83 |
| TRUSTCORP BK NA | Huntington | IN | 204 | 100.81 |
| INB NB NORTHWEST | Lafayette | IN | 204 | 692.64 |
| SUMMIT BK OF MUNCIE | Muncie | IN | 203 | 166.36 |
| UNION ST BK | Carmel | IN | 203 | 210.76 |
| SUMMIT BK CLINTON CITY | Frankfort | IN | 202 | 128.28 |
| BANK ONE NA | Indianapolis | IN | 201 | 4,170.60 |
| SHIPSHEWANA ST BK | Shipshewana | IN | 200 | 146.95 |
| WEST DES MOINES ST BK | West Des Moines | IA | 292 | 265.12 |
| DAVENPORT B&TC | Davenport | IA | 274 | 1,824.91 |
| FIRST NB IOWA CITY IOWA | Iowa City | IA | 259 | 304.34 |
| CITIZENS FIRST NB | Storm Lake | IA | 253 | 140.73 |

|  |  |  | | |
|---|---|---|---|---|
| UNION B&TC | Ottumwa | IA | 242 | 158.40 |
| FARMERS ST SVG BK | Independence | IA | 239 | 100.53 |
| FIRST NB | Ames | IA | 234 | 214.54 |
| FIRST AMERICAN ST BK | Fort Dodge | IA | 232 | 107.17 |
| WATERLOO SVG BK | Waterloo | IA | 225 | 264.90 |
| JASPER COUNTY SVG BK | Newton | IA | 224 | 119.20 |
| HILLS B&TC | Hills | IA | 218 | 302.21 |
| CENTRAL ST BK | Muscatine | IA | 217 | 205.81 |
| SHELBY COUNTY ST BK | Harlan | IA | 215 | 107.07 |
| MONTICELLO ST BK | Monticello | IA | 213 | 193.25 |
| CHEROKEE ST BK | Cherokee | IA | 208 | 118.27 |
| CITIZENS NB OF CHARLES | Charles City | IA | 202 | 113.65 |
| VALLEY NB | Des Moines | IA | 201 | 412.54 |
| COUNTRY HILL BK | Lenexa | KS | 258 | 102.60 |
| CITIZENS B&TC | Manhattan | KS | 256 | 109.42 |
| ARMY NB | Fort Leavenworth | KS | 249 | 114.80 |
| BANK IV PITTSBURG NA | Pittsburg | KS | 241 | 108.93 |
| FIRST NB OF LAWRENCE | Lawrence | KS | 237 | 134.40 |
| COLLEGE BOULEVARD NB | Overland Park | KS | 212 | 175.85 |
| UNION NB&TC OF MANHATTAN | Manhattan | KS | 211 | 155.45 |
| AMERICAN ST B&TC | Great Bend | KS | 209 | 105.17 |
| FIRST NB IN WICHITA | Wichita | KS | 208 | 813.90 |

*Continued*

153

| Name | City | State | IDC Rank | Assets (Mill. $) |
|------|------|-------|----------|------------------|
| FIRST CITY B&TC | Hopkinsville | KY | 279 | 173.08 |
| KENTUCKY FARMS BK CATLETTSBURG | Catlettsburg | KY | 275 | 111.11 |
| CITIZENS B&TC | Elizabethtown | KY | 272 | 230.97 |
| BANK OF ASHLAND | Ashland | KY | 256 | 111.46 |
| SOVRAN BK | Hopkinsville | KY | 248 | 200.61 |
| FIRST KENTUCKY TC | Louisville | KY | 246 | 141.78 |
| CITIZENS FIDELITY B&TC OLDHAM | La Grange | KY | 239 | 134.91 |
| FARMERS NB OF DANVILLE | Danville | KY | 239 | 122.40 |
| FARMERS B&TC | Bardstown | KY | 238 | 107.97 |
| FIFTH THIRD BK BOONE CITY | Florence | KY | 235 | 165.60 |
| PEOPLES BK OF MURRAY | Murray | KY | 230 | 155.15 |
| OWENSBORO NB | Owensboro | KY | 230 | 347.63 |
| BANK OF MURRAY | Murray | KY | 228 | 212.67 |
| NEW FARMERS ND OF GLASGOW | Glasgow | KY | 228 | 115.74 |
| HARLAN NB | Harlan | KY | 226 | 101.79 |
| PEOPLES FIRST NB&TC | Paducah | KY | 226 | 368.89 |
| STAR BK KENTON COUNTY | Covington | KY | 220 | 255.97 |
| FIRST GUARANTY NB | Martin | KY | 219 | 104.31 |
| FIFTH THIRD BK CAMPBELL COUNTY NA | Fort Thomas | KY | 218 | 176.11 |
| CITIZENS FIDELITY B&TC | Winchester | KY | 212 | 112.30 |
| CITIZENS ST BK | Owensboro | KY | 210 | 243.31 |
| BANK OF MARSHALL COUNTY | Benton | KY | 210 | 131.65 |
| BANK OF WHITESBURG | Whitesburg | KY | 209 | 123.91 |

154

# Top Rated U.S. Banks

|  |  |  | | |
|---|---|---|---|---|
| BOURBON-AGRCULTURAL DEPOSIT B&TC | Paris | KY | 207 | 132.23 |
| CENTRAL B&TC | Owensboro | KY | 207 | 197.84 |
| CITIZENS NB OF SOMERSET | Somerset | KY | 206 | 156.98 |
| CITIZENS B&TC | Paducah | KY | 206 | 437.87 |
| FIRST ST BK | Greenville | KY | 204 | 115.85 |
| CITIZENS UNION BK | Shelbyville | KY | 203 | 135.79 |
| STAR BK NA CAMPBELL CITY | Newport | KY | 203 | 171.72 |
| FIRST NB OF PIKEVILLE | Pikeville | KY | 202 | 229.05 |
| FARMERS B&TC OF MADISONVILLE | Madisonville | KY | 202 | 165.85 |
| MID AMERICAN B&TC OF LOUISVILLE | Louisville | KY | 201 | 882.51 |
| MONTGOMERY & TRADERS B&TC | Mt Sterling | KY | 200 | 123.42 |
| FARMERS B&TC CAPITAL TC | Frankfort | KY | 200 | 341.26 |
| METAIRIE B&TC | Metairie | LA | 231 | 183.40 |
| BASTROP NB | Bastrop | LA | 212 | 107.60 |
| EVANGELINE B&TC | Ville Platte | LA | 208 | 113.36 |
| FIRST NB IN DERIDDER | Deridder | LA | 207 | 101.65 |
| SAINT BERNARD B&TC | Arabi | LA | 204 | 150.08 |
| CAMDEN NB | Camden | ME | 256 | 269.31 |
| BAR HARBOR BK GUARANTY & TC | Bar Harbor | ME | 207 | 186.67 |
| FIRST NB OF SAINT MARYS | Leonardtown | MD | 281 | 185.28 |
| CITIZENS NB | Laurel | MD | 272 | 375.59 |
| CHASE BK OF MARYLAND | Baltimore | MD | 272 | 1,149.27 |

Continued

| Name | City | State | IDC Rank | Assets (Mill. $) |
|---|---|---|---|---|
| CENTREVILLE NB OF MARYLAND | Centreville | MD | 267 | 118.53 |
| MERCANTILE SAFE DEPOSIT & TC | Baltimore | MD | 264 | 1,774.03 |
| BANK OF SOUTHERN MARYLAND | La Plata | MD | 257 | 113.60 |
| CHESTERTOWN BK OF MARYLAND | Chestertown | MD | 254 | 142.27 |
| COUNTY BK GUARANTY & TC | Elkton | MD | 251 | 204.10 |
| WESTMINSTER B&TC CARROLL COUNTY | Westminster | MD | 236 | 185.26 |
| PENINSULA BK | Princess Anne | MD | 233 | 258.62 |
| NATIONAL BANK OF CAMBRIDGE | Cambridge | MD | 231 | 117.31 |
| FARMERS NB OF MARYLAND | Annapolis | MD | 231 | 434.64 |
| FREDERICK COUNTY NB OF FREDERICK | Frederick | MD | 228 | 274.93 |
| CALVIN B TAYLOR BK GUARANTY COMPANY | Berlin | MD | 222 | 173.69 |
| FREDERICKTOWN B&TC | Frederick | MD | 220 | 186.06 |
| CITIZENS BK OF MARYLAND | Riverdale | MD | 220 | 2,299.37 |
| CARROLLTON BK OF BALTIMORE | Baltimore | MD | 218 | 173.21 |
| TANEYTOWN B&TC | Taneytown | MD | 214 | 133.95 |
| QUEENSTOWN BK OF MARYLAND | Queenstown | MD | 213 | 106.33 |
| TALBOT BK | Easton | MD | 213 | 170.85 |
| FARMERS & MECHANICS BK | Frederick | MD | 213 | 511.89 |
| FIRST UNITED NB&TC | Oakland | MD | 212 | 318.00 |
| BANK OF GLEN BURNIE | Glen Burnie | MD | 211 | 135.34 |
| COMMERCIAL & FARMERS BK | Ellicott City | MD | 207 | 100.70 |

# Top Rated U.S. Banks

| Bank | City | State | Rating |
|------|------|-------|-------|
| SHAWMUT BK OF HAMPSHIRE COUNTY | Amherst | MA | 191.57 |
| BAYBANK FIRST EASTHAMPTON | Easthampton | MA | 108.44 |
| SHAWMUT BK OF FRANKLIN COUNTY | Greenfield | MA | 133.22 |
| SHAWMUT FIRST B&TC | Springfield | MA | 559.60 |
| UNITED STATES TC | Boston | MA | 1,395.62 |
| STATE STREET B&TC | Boston | MA | 10,390.93 |
| BYRON CENTER ST BK | Byron Center | MI | 129.89 |
| NBD F&M BK NA | Benton Harbor | MI | 259.96 |
| OLD KENT BK OF GRAND HAVEN | Grand Haven | MI | 341.36 |
| OLD KENT BK SOUTHEAST | Trenton | MI | 280.25 |
| FIRST OF AMERICA BK—PLYMOUTH NA | Plymouth | MI | 101.05 |
| WARREN BK | Warren | MI | 365.68 |
| OLD KENT BK OF GAYLORD | Gaylord | MI | 150.20 |
| FIRST NB&TC | Petoskey | MI | 178.36 |
| CHELSEA ST BK | Chelsea | MI | 118.90 |
| MICHIGAN NB-FARMINGTON | Farmington Hills | MI | 10,114.10 |
| OLD KENT BK OF HOLLAND | Holland | MI | 296.48 |
| NBD SAGINAW | Saginaw | MI | 181.40 |
| FIRST OF AMERICA BK-CENTRAL | Lansing | MI | 598.71 |
| NBD GRAND HAVEN | Grand Haven | MI | 202.88 |
| PEOPLES ST BK | Hamtramck | MI | 135.40 |
| NBD GRAND RAPIDS NA | Grand Rapids | MI | 1,334.20 |
| OLD KENT BK OF BIG RAPIDS | Big Rapids | MI | 118.55 |
| FMB-FIRST MICHIGAN BK | Zeeland | MI | 694.69 |

*Continued*

157

| Name | City | State | IDC Rank | Assets (Mill. $) |
|------|------|-------|----------|------------------|
| FIRST OF AMERICA BK-ANN ARBOR | Ann Arbor | MI | 230 | 607.22 |
| BANK ONE | Sturgis | MI | 229 | 159.34 |
| NBD CADILLAC BK | Cadillac | MI | 227 | 408.40 |
| OLD KENT B&TC | Grand Rapids | MI | 227 | 3,202.28 |
| CHEMICAL B&TC | Midland | MI | 226 | 473.81 |
| FIRST OF AMERICA BK-MICHIGAN NA | Kalamazoo | MI | 225 | 1,318.62 |
| OXFORD BK | Oxford | MI | 225 | 132.31 |
| OLD KENT BK OF BRIGHTON | Brighton | MI | 225 | 280.04 |
| CITY B&TC NA | Jackson | MI | 222 | 380.73 |
| HILLSDALE COUNTY NB | Hillsdale | MI | 221 | 109.08 |
| SECURITY B&TC | Southgate | MI | 217 | 1,553.35 |
| CITIZENS NB OF CHEBOYGAN | Cheboygan | MI | 216 | 137.05 |
| BANK OF FENTON NA | Fenton | MI | 215 | 106.11 |
| FIRST NB IN HOWELL | Howell | MI | 215 | 129.20 |
| UNITED SVG BK OF TECUMSEH | Tecumseh | MI | 214 | 184.71 |
| STATE BK OF FRASER | Fraser | MI | 214 | 140.51 |
| FIRST AMERICA BK | Wayne | MI | 212 | 109.98 |
| OLD KENT BK OF PETOSKEY | Petoskey | MI | 212 | 131.49 |
| FIRST AMERICA BK-MONROE | Monroe | MI | 211 | 138.08 |
| FIRST OF AMERICA BK LIVINGSTON | Howell | MI | 210 | 134.51 |
| FIRST NB IRON MOUNTAIN | Iron Mountain | MI | 208 | 114.80 |
| LIBERTY ST B&TC | Troy | MI | 208 | 483.50 |
| NBD GENESEE BK | Flint | MI | 207 | 1095.75 |

158

|  |  |  | | |
|---|---|---|---|---|
| STATE BK OF STANDISH | Standish | MI | 207 | 116.51 |
| FMB-LUMBERMANS BK | Muskegon | MI | 203 | 301.81 |
| MONROE B&TC | Monroe | MI | 203 | 490.04 |
| FIRST MACOMB BK | Mt Clemens | MI | 202 | 398.24 |
| SECURITY BK OF MONROE | Monroe | MI | 202 | 279.91 |
| OLD KENT BK GRAND TRAVERSE | Traverse City | MI | 202 | 362.50 |
| STATE BK | Fenton | MI | 201 | 156.02 |
| OLD KENT BK OF CADILLAC | Cadillac | MI | 201 | 108.06 |
| IDS B&TC | Minneapolis | MN | 282 | 148.83 |
| EASTERN HEIGHTS ST BK | St Paul | MN | 245 | 257.54 |
| FIRST WESTERN BK ST LOUIS | St Louis Park | MN | 241 | 138.71 |
| FIRST BANK IN ANOKA | Anoka | MN | 229 | 227.89 |
| NORTHWEST BK MANKATO NA | Mankato | MN | 227 | 297.63 |
| WINONA NAT&SAV BK | Winona | MN | 227 | 120.42 |
| WESTERN ST BK OF SAINT PAUL | Saint Paul | MN | 219 | 117.74 |
| FIRST NB OF BEMIDJI | Bemidji | MN | 208 | 171.74 |
| NORTHWEST BK DULUTH NA | Duluth | MN | 207 | 377.72 |
| MARQUETTE BK GOLDEN VALLEY | Golden Valley | MN | 201 | 115.18 |
| CITIZENS B&TC | Belzoni | MS | 229 | 151.49 |
| BANK OF NEW ALBANY | New Albany | MS | 227 | 140.08 |
| FIRST NB OF PONTOTOC | Pontotoc | MS | 220 | 101.90 |
| NATIONAL BK OF CMRC CORINTH | Corinth | MS | 209 | 105.93 |
| NATIONAL BK OF CMRC OF MS | Starkville | MS | 204 | 364.63 |

*Continued*

159

| Name | City | State | IDC Rank | Assets (Mill. $) |
|------|------|-------|----------|------------------|
| INVESTORS FIDUCIARY TC | Kansas City | MO | 279 | 486.15 |
| MIDLAND BK | Kansas City | MO | 267 | 285.05 |
| JEFFERSON B&TC | Eureka | MO | 257 | 190.73 |
| COMMERCE BK POPLAR BLUFF NA | Poplar Bluff | MO | 244 | 116.27 |
| BANK OF WASHINGTON | Washington | MO | 234 | 170.22 |
| EMPIRE BK | Springfield | MO | 232 | 193.05 |
| MERCANTILE BK FRANKLIN COUNTY | Washington | MO | 231 | 112.63 |
| BANK OF ODESSA | Odessa | MO | 229 | 116.73 |
| JEFFERSON BK OF MISSOURI | Jefferson City | MO | 220 | 165.27 |
| COMMERCE BK OF SAINT CHARLES NA | St Peters | MO | 219 | 195.14 |
| FIRST NB | Kirksville | MO | 218 | 104.81 |
| BOONE COUNTY NB OF COLUMBIA | Columbia | MO | 218 | 372.69 |
| UNITED MISSOURI BK KANSAS CITY NA | Kansas City | MO | 216 | 2,078.14 |
| FIRST EXCHANGE BK OF CAPE GIRARDEAU | Cape Girardeau | MO | 214 | 117.13 |
| MERCANTILE BK SPRINGFIELD | Springfield | MO | 214 | 201.64 |
| FIRST BK | Creve Coeur | MO | 214 | 565.12 |
| SOUTHERN COMMERCIAL BK | St Louis | MO | 213 | 180.01 |
| BOATMENS NB OF SPRINGFIELD | Springfield | MO | 210 | 848.80 |
| JACKSON EXCHANGE B&TC | Jackson | MO | 210 | 166.73 |
| BOATSMENS FIRST NB | West Plains | MO | 207 | 143.42 |
| COMMERCE BK ST LOUIS NA | Clayton | MO | 207 | 2,112.73 |
| FIRST BK | Gladstone | MO | 204 | 221.19 |

|  |  |  | | |
|---|---|---|---|---|
| MERCANTILE BK OF FARMINGTON | Farmington | MO | 201 | 117.24 |
| EXCHANGE NB OF JEFFERSON | Jefferson City | MO | 200 | 247.95 |
| FIRST NB OF OMAHA | Omaha | NE | 254 | 1,439.98 |
| SOUTHWEST B&TC OF OMAHA | Omaha | NE | 233 | 134.08 |
| FIRST NB&TC COLUMBUS | Columbus | NE | 224 | 235.87 |
| NATIONAL BK OF CMRC TR & SA | Lincoln | NE | 213 | 550.47 |
| FIRSTIER BK NA | Norfolk | NE | 205 | 203.61 |
| FIVE POINTS BK | Grand Island | NE | 205 | 100.71 |
| CITIBANK NEVADA NA | Las Vegas | NV | 288 | 6,139.38 |
| NEVADA ST BK | Las Vegas | NV | 275 | 285.47 |
| FIRST INTERSTATE BK NEVADA NA | Reno | NV | 225 | 3,868.84 |
| AMERICAN BK OF COMMERCE | Las Vegas | NV | 223 | 116.06 |
| VALLEY BK OF NEVADA | Las Vegas | NV | 217 | 2,992.30 |
| FIRST DEPOSIT NB | Tilton | NH | 300 | 1,215.58 |
| PRINCETON BK & TC NA | Morristown | NJ | 283 | 177.30 |
| BESSEMER TC | Newark | NJ | 270 | 116.62 |
| VALLEY NB | Passaic | NJ | 269 | 1,845.37 |
| FIRST STATE BK | Howell Twp | NJ | 237 | 224.61 |
| COMMUNITY BK OF BERGEN COUNTY | Maywood | NJ | 236 | 114.32 |
| WOODSTOWN NB&TC | Woodstown | NJ | 230 | 176.72 |
| MINOTOLA NB | Vineland | NJ | 227 | 180.08 |
| SHREWSBURY ST BK | Shrewsbury | NJ | 218 | 127.80 |

*Continued*

| Name | City | State | IDC Rank | Assets (Mill. $) |
|---|---|---|---|---|
| NORTH PLAINFIELD ST BK | North Plainfield | NJ | 216 | 148.90 |
| UNITED COUNTIES TC | Cranford | NJ | 207 | 1,240.05 |
| PEAPACK GLADSTONE BK | Gladstone | NJ | 205 | 142.69 |
| LAKELAND ST BK | West Milford Twp | NJ | 203 | 165.06 |
| INDEPENDENCE BK OF NEW JERSEY | Allendale | NJ | 202 | 213.92 |
| FIRST INTERSTATE BK NA | Santa Fe | NM | 215 | 131.38 |
| WESTERN COMMERCE BK | Carlsbad | NM | 204 | 100.19 |
| GATEWAY ST BK | Dongan Hills | NY | 276 | 279.79 |
| WILBER NB | Oneonta | NY | 273 | 268.72 |
| FIDUCIARY TC | New York | NY | 273 | 204.05 |
| GLENS FALLS NB&TC | Glens Falls | NY | 264 | 430.63 |
| MERCHANTS BK OF NEW YORK | New York | NY | 260 | 621.42 |
| SUMITOMO TR&BKG CO USA | New York | NY | 257 | 777.74 |
| HUDSON VALLEY NB | Yonkers | NY | 247 | 275.72 |
| TRUSTCO BK NEW YORK | Schenectady | NY | 240 | 868.06 |
| KEY BK USA NA | Albany | NY | 239 | 318.74 |
| YASUDA B&TC USA | New York | NY | 239 | 521.33 |
| FIRST NB LONG ISLAND | Glen Head | NY | 239 | 311.11 |
| CANADIAN IMPERIAL BK OF CMRC | New York | NY | 235 | 426.99 |
| ADIRONDACK TC | Saratoga Springs | NY | 231 | 232.70 |
| NORSTAR BK OF UPSTATE NEW YORK | Albany | NY | 231 | 4,730.60 |

162

|  |  |  | | |
|---|---|---|---|---|
| CITY NB&TC | Gloversville | NY | 228 | 135.43 |
| MITSUBISHI TR & BANKING CORPORATION | New York | NY | 226 | 327.42 |
| WYOMING COUNTY BK | Warsaw | NY | 222 | 191.31 |
| ORANGE COUNTY TC | Middletown | NY | 221 | 104.72 |
| LTCB TC | New York | NY | 221 | 1,122.48 |
| TOMPKINS COUNTY TC | Ithaca | NY | 220 | 371.02 |
| FIRST NB JEFFERSONVILLE | Jeffersonville | NY | 220 | 139.96 |
| ONEIDA VALLEY NB OF ONEIDA | Oneida | NY | 217 | 156.63 |
| MITSUI TR BK USA | New York | NY | 217 | 283.78 |
| STERLING NB&TC OF NEW YORK | New York | NY | 211 | 504.61 |
| FIRST NB OF GLENS FALLS | Glens Falls | NY | 209 | 626.42 |
| KEY BK OF WESTERN NEW YORK NA | Buffalo | NY | 208 | 1,304.33 |
| STATE BK OF LONG ISLAND | New Hyde Park | NY | 208 | 230.78 |
| BANK OF CASTILE | Castile | NY | 204 | 104.60 |
| NORSTAR BK | Hempstead | NY | 203 | 2,931.46 |
| NATIONAL BK OF GENEVA | Geneva | NY | 202 | 132.63 |
| UNION ST BK | Nanuet | NY | 201 | 273.26 |
| CHINESE AMERICAN BK | New York | NY | 201 | 671.54 |
| BANK OF GRANITE | Granite Falls | NC | 298 | 313.15 |
| REPUBLIC B&TC | Charlotte | NC | 247 | 190.75 |
| LEXINGTON ST BK | Lexington | NC | 236 | 292.37 |
| SECURITY B&TC | Salisbury | NC | 234 | 357.53 |
| WACHOVIA B&TC NA | Winston-Salem | NC | 234 | 15,492.28 |
| FIDELITY BK | Fuquay-Varina | NC | 231 | 225.93 |

*Continued*

163

# Like A Bulging Wall

| Name | City | State | IDC Rank | Assets (Mill. $) |
|---|---|---|---|---|
| FIRST NB OF SHELBY | Shelby | NC | 227 | 230.74 |
| YADKIN VALLEY B&TC | Elkin | NC | 221 | 164.60 |
| FIRST CHARTER NB | Concord | NC | 212 | 234.50 |
| PEOPLES B&TC | Rocky Mount | NC | 203 | 1,159.80 |
| FIRST NB OF REIDSVILLE | Reidsville | NC | 201 | 131.98 |
| PEOPLES BK | Newton | NC | 200 | 151.98 |
| STATE BK OF FARGO | Fargo | ND | 209 | 111.44 |
| PARK NB | Newark | OH | 296 | 581.72 |
| WORLD FINANCIAL NETWORK NB | Whitehall | OH | 296 | 577.78 |
| COMERICA BK-MIDWEST NA | Toledo | OH | 287 | 269.25 |
| SECURITY NB&TC | Springfield | OH | 274 | 393.41 |
| CITY LOAN BK | Columbus | OH | 264 | 276.27 |
| FIFTH THIRD BK OF SOUTHERN OHIO | Hillsboro | OH | 264 | 252.01 |
| STATE B&TC | Defiance | OH | 258 | 161.72 |
| FIFTH THIRD BK | Cincinnati | OH | 253 | 4,080.85 |
| STAR BK NA TROY | Troy | OH | 245 | 227.45 |
| FIRST NB OF ASHLAND | Ashland | OH | 244 | 144.70 |
| BANK ONE DAYTON NA | Dayton | OH | 244 | 2,454.56 |
| OLD PHOENIX NB OF MEDINA | Medina | OH | 241 | 307.38 |
| FIFTH THIRD BK MIAMI VALLEY NA | Piqua | OH | 240 | 386.48 |
| CENTRAL TC NORTHEAST OHIO NA | Canton | OH | 239 | 988.22 |

164

# Top Rated U.S. Banks

| | | | |
|---|---|---|---|
| FIRST NB | Dayton | OH | 237 | 1,114.12 |
| THIRD NB OF SANDUSKY | Sandusky | OH | 235 | 163.16 |
| MONOGRAM BK USA | Cincinnati | OH | 232 | 803.21 |
| NATIONAL CITY BK | Akron | OH | 229 | 1,125.79 |
| LEBANON CITIZENS NB | Lebanon | OH | 228 | 206.35 |
| CITIZENS BKG CO | Salineville | OH | 226 | 274.18 |
| FARMERS & MERCHANTS ST BK | Archbold | OH | 223 | 288.88 |
| BANK ONE DOVER NA | Dover | OH | 223 | 260.67 |
| FIRST NB BARNESVILLE | Barnesville | OH | 223 | 135.25 |
| OHIO CITIZENS BK | Toledo | OH | 220 | 1,153.58 |
| CENTRAL TC OF SOUTHEASTERN OHIO NA | Marietta | OH | 218 | 232.65 |
| FIRST NB | Orrville | OH | 218 | 126.88 |
| FIRST NB SOUTHWESTERN OH | Monroe | OH | 218 | 815.62 |
| RICHLAND TC | Mansfield | OH | 215 | 219.72 |
| PEOPLES BK CO | Coldwater | OH | 214 | 116.58 |
| STAR BK NA CINCINNATI | Cincinnati | OH | 213 | 3,083.24 |
| FIRST NB OF ZANESVILLE | Zanesville | OH | 213 | 265.50 |
| FIFTH THIRD BK OF WESTERN OHIO NA | Wapakoneta | OH | 212 | 118.66 |
| CITIZENS COMMERCIAL B&TC | Celina | OH | 210 | 170.19 |
| SOCIETY NB | Cleveland | OH | 209 | 7,677.75 |
| ELYRIA SVG & TR NB | Elyria | OH | 207 | 444.33 |
| COMMERCIAL BK | Delphos | OH | 207 | 120.06 |
| FIRST CITIZENS NB OF UPPER SANDUSKY | Upper Sandusky | OH | 205 | 101.07 |
| STAR BK SOUTH CENTRAL OHIO | Portsmouth | OH | 204 | 163.67 |

Continued

165

| Name | City | State | IDC Rank | Assets (Mill. $) |
|---|---|---|---|---|
| BANK ONE AKRON NA | Akron | OH | 204 | 1,366.40 |
| WAYNE COUNTY NB OF WOOSTER | Wooster | OH | 203 | 238.64 |
| BANK ONE COSHOCTON NA | Coshocton | OH | 203 | 180.23 |
| CITIZENS BKG CO | Sandusky | OH | 203 | 203.01 |
| STAR BK NA SIDNEY OHIO | Sidney | OH | 202 | 219.89 |
| DELAWARE COUNTY BK | Delaware | OH | 201 | 229.74 |
| SECURITY BK | Tulsa | OK | 275 | 125.98 |
| FIRST INTERSTATE BK OKLAHOMA NA | Oklahoma City | OK | 273 | 841.80 |
| FIRST NB&TC MC ALESTER | Mc Alester | OK | 229 | 317.50 |
| FIRST INTERSTATE BK OREGON NA | Portland | OR | 240 | 6,158.79 |
| CENTENNIAL BK | Eugene | OR | 234 | 104.44 |
| UNITED STATES NB | Portland | OR | 229 | 10,810.38 |
| ROYAL BK OF PENNSYLVANIA | King of Purssia | PA | 290 | 301.94 |
| FIRST NB OF LEECHBURG | Leechburg | PA | 275 | 116.58 |
| FIRST B&TC | Mechanicsburg | PA | 265 | 159.11 |
| FARMERS TC | Carlisle | PA | 265 | 329.03 |
| COUNTY NB OF MONTROSE | Montrose | PA | 256 | 170.30 |
| BANK OF PENNSLYVANIA | Reading | PA | 256 | 811.03 |
| NATIONAL BK OF BOYERTOWN | Boyertown | PA | 250 | 561.05 |
| NATIONAL BK OF THE MAIN LINE | Wayne | PA | 250 | 155.08 |

166

## Top Rated U.S. Banks

|  |  |  | | |
|---|---|---|---|---|
| PEOPLES BK | Oxford | PA | 247 | 119.74 |
| FULTON BK | Lancaster | PA | 246 | 1075.07 |
| FARMERS FIRST BK | Lititz | PA | 245 | 664.10 |
| ADAMS COUNTY NB | Cumberland Twp | PA | 243 | 400.35 |
| MID PENN BK | Millersburg | PA | 243 | 156.45 |
| DENVER NB | Denver | PA | 243 | 165.34 |
| WILLIAMSPORT NB | Williamsport | PA | 239 | 202.78 |
| EPHRATA NB | Ephrata | PA | 237 | 221.60 |
| DEPOSIT BK | Du Bois | PA | 236 | 282.81 |
| UNION NB&TC | Souderton | PA | 236 | 576.48 |
| BLUE BALL NB | Blue Ball | PA | 233 | 286.31 |
| PEOPLES NB SUSQUEHANNA | Hallstead | PA | 233 | 104.25 |
| HARLEYSVILLE NB&TC | Harleysville | PA | 233 | 381.01 |
| COMMONWEALTH NB | Harrisburg | PA | 226 | 1,425.97 |
| PEOPLES BK OF UNITY | Plum Boro | PA | 226 | 170.75 |
| FIRST NB OF PALMERTON | Palmerton | PA | 225 | 177.36 |
| WAYNE COUNTY B&TC | Honesdale | PA | 224 | 163.25 |
| PEOPLES NB OF CENTRAL PENNSYLVANIA | State College | PA | 224 | 303.60 |
| MID-STATE B&TC | Altoona | PA | 223 | 949.82 |
| FIRST NB&TC | Waynesboro | PA | 222 | 174.19 |
| COUNTY NB | Clearfield | PA | 221 | 238.63 |
| LEBANON VALLEY NB | Lebanon | PA | 221 | 531.19 |
| CCNB BK NA | New Cumberland | PA | 219 | 858.61 |
| THIRD NB&TC | Scranton | PA | 217 | 411.53 |

*Continued*

167

# Like A Bulging Wall

| Name | City | State | IDC Rank | Assets (Mill. $) |
|------|------|-------|----------|------------------|
| PENNSYLVANIA NB&TC | Pottsville | PA | 217 | 864.16 |
| OLD FORGE BK | Old Forge | PA | 217 | 108.49 |
| BANK OF LANCASTER COUNTY NA | Strasburg | PA | 216 | 436.43 |
| JUNIATA VALLEY BK | Mifflintown | PA | 216 | 159.51 |
| PENN CENTRAL NB | Huntingdon | PA | 216 | 156.41 |
| FIRST NB OF WESTERN PENNSYLVANIA | New Castle | PA | 215 | 320.09 |
| HAZLETON NB | Nuremberg | PA | 213 | 438.01 |
| CONTINENTAL BK | Norristown | PA | 213 | 4,527.92 |
| MARINE BK | Warren | PA | 212 | 1,869.36 |
| MERCHANTS NB OF BANGOR | Bangor | PA | 212 | 104.53 |
| CLEARFIELD B&TC | Clearfield | PA | 211 | 119.98 |
| PHILADELPHIA NB | Ardmore | PA | 210 | 10,474.47 |
| FIRST NB&TC | Newtown | PA | 209 | 214.29 |
| SNYDER COUNTY TC | Selinsgrove | PA | 209 | 158.22 |
| HOLLIDAYSBURG TC | Hollidaysburg | PA | 208 | 175.29 |
| CHAMBERSBURG TC | Chambersburg | PA | 208 | 148.31 |
| DAUPHIN DEPOSIT B&TC | Harrisburg | PA | 208 | 2,466.94 |
| HAMLIN B&TC | Smethport | PA | 207 | 120.38 |
| NORTHERN CENTRAL BK | Williamsport | PA | 207 | 775.30 |
| UNION NAT MOUNT JOY BK | Mount Joy | PA | 206 | 118.40 |
| FIRST NB OF BERWICK | Berwick | PA | 205 | 140.67 |
| FIRST BK OF GREATER PITTSTON | Pittston | PA | 204 | 134.30 |

168

# Top Rated U.S. Banks

|  |  |  | | |
|---|---|---|---|---|
| FIRST COLUMBIA BK&TC | Bloomsburg | PA | 204 | 136.70 |
| SWINEFORD NB OF MIDDLEBURG | Middleburg | PA | 203 | 116.78 |
| FARMERS & MERCHANTS TC CHAMBERSBURG | Chambersburg | PA | 203 | 245.98 |
| JERSEY SHORE ST BK | Jersey Shore | PA | 202 | 138.08 |
| HOME L&IA | Providence | RI | 209 | 235.07 |
| CITIZENS & SOUTHERN NB | Charleston | SC | 230 | 4,145.53 |
| CONWAY NB | Conway | SC | 210 | 212.76 |
| BRANCH BK GUARANTY & TC SC | Greenville | SC | 208 | 384.96 |
| ANCHOR BK | Myrtle Beach | SC | 205 | 128.10 |
| NCNB NB OF SOUTH CAROLINA | Columbia | SC | 202 | 5,026.72 |
| REPUBLIC NB | Columbia | SC | 200 | 445.16 |
| CITIBANK SOUTH DAKOTA NA | Sioux Falls | SD | 274 | 9,162.49 |
| HURLEY ST BK | Sioux Falls | SD | 241 | 268.07 |
| DIAL BK | Sioux Falls | SD | 230 | 133.73 |
| PIONEER B&TC | Belle Fourche | SD | 208 | 126.73 |
| NORWEST BK SOUTH DAKOTA NA | Sioux Falls | SD | 206 | 2,063.48 |
| FIRST DAKOTA NB | Yankton | SD | 206 | 140.17 |
| BANK OF ROANE COUNTY | Harriman | TN | 270 | 130.55 |
| MERCHANTS ST BK | Humboldt | TN | 262 | 111.66 |
| FIRST NB OF MCMINNVILLE | McMinnville | TN | 258 | 138.85 |
| CITIZENS BK | Carthage | TN | 255 | 170.69 |
| VALLEY FIDELITY B&TC | Knoxville | TN | 241 | 528.61 |

*Continued*

| Name | City | State | IDC Rank | Assets (Mill. $) |
|---|---|---|---|---|
| CITIZENS BK | Elizabethton | TN | 241 | 128.91 |
| SOVRAN BK GREENEVILLE | Greeneville | TN | 240 | 134.08 |
| FIRST NB OF PULASKI | Pulaski | TN | 239 | 161.65 |
| COMMERCIAL B&TC | Paris | TN | 237 | 140.34 |
| BARRETVILLE B&TC | Barretville | TN | 230 | 188.53 |
| NASHVILLE BK OF COMMERCE | Nashville | TN | 226 | 118.50 |
| FIRST NB&TC ATHEN | Athens | TN | 219 | 121.51 |
| FIRST CITIZENS BK | Cleveland | TN | 218 | 113.90 |
| GREENE COUNTY BK | Greeneville | TN | 218 | 213.58 |
| CITY B&TC | McMinnville | TN | 217 | 189.36 |
| NBC KNOXVILLE BK | Knoxville | TN | 207 | 108.76 |
| CITIZENS UNION BK | Rogersville | TN | 206 | 205.48 |
| CITIZENS BK OF BLOUNT COUNTY | Maryville | TN | 205 | 119.77 |
| NATIONAL BK OF COMMERCE | Memphis | TN | 205 | 1,702.48 |
| MERCHANTS BK | Cleveland | TN | 204 | 119.00 |
| UNION BK | Pulaski | TN | 204 | 100.90 |
| FIRST FARMERS & MERCHANTS N | Columbia | TN | 202 | 277.04 |
| TEXAS COMMERCE BK—MIDLAND | Midland | TX | 284 | 130.98 |
| FIRST ST BK | Athens | TX | 247 | 138.84 |
| FRIENDSWOOD BK | Friendswood | TX | 245 | 135.52 |
| LIBERTY NB IN PARIS | Paris | TX | 242 | 148.10 |

170

|  |  |  | | |
|---|---|---|---|---|
| PARK NB OF HOUSTON | Houston | TX | 233 | 126.50 |
| FIRST AMERICAN BK | Bryan | TX | 224 | 210.74 |
| KLEBERG FIRST NB | Kingsville | TX | 224 | 154.57 |
| COMPASS BK | Houston | TX | 220 | 222.94 |
| WESTSIDE BK | San Antonio | TX | 219 | 115.92 |
| FIRST NB OF BAY CITY | Bay City | TX | 219 | 144.27 |
| FIRST ST B&TC | Carthage | TX | 217 | 127.96 |
| NCNB TEXAS NB | Dallas | TX | 216 | 34,073.24 |
| FIRST B&TC | Groves | TX | 214 | 218.18 |
| TEXAS COMMERCE BK—CONROE NA | Conroe | TX | 210 | 115.68 |
| FIRST ST&TC | Mission | TX | 208 | 286.81 |
| HIBERNIA NB IN TEXAS | Dallas | TX | 203 | 911.04 |
| USAA CREDIT CD BK | Salt Lake City | UT | 300 | 102.85 |
| AMERICAN GENERAL FINANCIAL CENTER | Salt Lake City | UT | 256 | 337.25 |
| MERRILL LYNCH NAT FINANCIAL | Salt Lake City | UT | 227 | 282.58 |
| UNION BK | Morrisville | VT | 240 | 114.54 |
| CALEDONIA NB OF DANVILLE | Danville | VT | 229 | 104.47 |
| COMMUNITY NB | Derby | VT | 221 | 130.75 |
| FRANKLIN—LAMOILLE BK | St Albans | VT | 221 | 257.74 |
| LYNDONVILLE SVG B&TC | Lyndonville | VT | 212 | 127.58 |
| MERCHANTS BK | Burlington | VT | 201 | 584.16 |
| CENTRAL FIDELITY BK NA | Richmond | VA | 300 | 115.64 |

*Continued*

171

# Like A Bulging Wall

| Name | City | State | IDC Rank | Assets (Mill. $) |
|------|------|-------|----------|------------------|
| BANK OF SOUTHSIDE VIRGINIA | Carson | VA | 288 | 155.54 |
| FARMERS & MERCHANTS BK | Onley | VA | 282 | 127.48 |
| MIDDLEBURG NB | Middleburg | VA | 278 | 105.25 |
| PEOPLES BK OF DANVILLE | Danville | VA | 267 | 218.79 |
| CITIZENS & FARMERS BK | West Point | VA | 265 | 146.75 |
| PATRICK HENRY NB | Bassett | VA | 262 | 186.45 |
| FIRST VIRGINIA BK SHENANDOAH | Woodstock | VA | 252 | 161.58 |
| AMERICAN NB&TC | Danville | VA | 246 | 200.38 |
| GEORGE MASON BK | Fairfax | VA | 244 | 170.86 |
| FIRST VIRGINIA BK | Fairfax City | VA | 240 | 2,115.45 |
| FARMERS & MERCHANTS NB | Winchester | VA | 234 | 451.07 |
| FIRST VIRGINIA BK COLONIAL | Richmond | VA | 233 | 293.33 |
| FIRST VIRGINIA BK SOUTHSIDE | Farmville | VA | 231 | 116.04 |
| BURKE & HERBERT B&TC | Alexandria | VA | 227 | 342.96 |
| NATIONAL BK OF BLACKSBURG | Blacksburg | VA | 227 | 168.18 |
| SECOND NB | Culpeper | VA | 226 | 179.22 |
| FIRST NB OF ROCKY MOUNT | Rocky Mount | VA | 219 | 127.39 |
| BANK OF TAZEWELL COUNTY | Tazewell | VA | 218 | 148.34 |
| PIEDMONT TR BK | Martinsville | VA | 212 | 359.25 |
| UNION B&TC | Bowling Green | VA | 211 | 183.71 |
| PLANTERS B&TC OF VIRGINIA | Staunton | VA | 211 | 224.60 |
| SOVRAN BK NA | Richmond | VA | 210 | 14,637.50 |

# Top Rated U.S. Banks

|  |  |  | | |
|---|---|---|---|---|
| DOMINION BK SHENANDOAH VALLEY NA | Bridgewater | VA | 209 | 703.17 |
| FAUQUIER NB OF WARRENTON | Warrenton | VA | 208 | 125.69 |
| FIRST VA BK—PIEDMONT | Lynchburg | VA | 205 | 155.58 |
| FIRST VIRGINIA BK FRANKLIN | Rocky Mount | VA | 203 | 113.07 |
| DOMINION BK NA | Roanoke County | VA | 201 | 4,877.33 |
| OLD POINT NB OF PHOEBUS | Hampton | VA | 200 | 242.06 |
| CITY BANK | Lynnwood | WA | 300 | 199.13 |
| SAN JUAN COUNTY BK | Friday Harbor | WA | 265 | 103.59 |
| FRONTIER BK | Everett | WA | 253 | 272.29 |
| NORTHWEST NB | Vancouver | WA | 245 | 166.83 |
| SECURITY PACIFIC BK WASHINGTON NA | Seattle | WA | 241 | 8,625.88 |
| CASHMERE VALLEY BK | Cashmere | WA | 238 | 169.25 |
| SKAGIT ST BK | Burlington | WA | 235 | 195.59 |
| FIRST INDEPENDENT BK | Vancouver | WA | 229 | 391.63 |
| CENTRAL WASHINGTON BK | Wenatchee | WA | 213 | 106.47 |
| BELLINGHAM NB | Bellingham | WA | 212 | 283.54 |
| FIRST NB OF MORGANTOWN | Morgantown | WV | 276 | 353.89 |
| SECURITY NB & TC | Wheeling | WV | 251 | 217.56 |
| MCDOWELL COUNTY NB WELCH | Welch | WV | 227 | 111.56 |
| RALEIGH COUNTY NB | Beckley | WV | 226 | 195.89 |
| UNITED NB—CENTRAL | Glenville | WV | 219 | 176.55 |
| NATIONAL BK OF LOGAN | Logan | WV | 216 | 157.07 |
| UNION NB OF CLARKSBURG | Clarksburg | WV | 215 | 268.63 |

*Continued*

173

| Name | City | State | IDC Rank | Assets (Mill. $) |
|---|---|---|---|---|
| ONE VALLEY BK MERCER COUNTY | Princeton | WV | 209 | 157.64 |
| BOONE NB OF MADISON | Madison | WV | 207 | 111.16 |
| CENTRAL NB OF BUCKHANNO | Buckhannon | WV | 206 | 174.28 |
| WHEELING DOLLAR BK | Wheeling | WV | 201 | 297.36 |
| MATEWAN NB | Matewan | WV | 201 | 292.02 |
| BANK OF WEIRTON | Weirton | WV | 201 | 172.94 |
| NATIONAL EXCH B&TC OF FOND DU LAC | Fond Du Lac | WI | 275 | 237.53 |
| WOOD COUNTY NB&TC | Wisconsin Rapids | WI | 253 | 134.09 |
| BANK OF BURLINGTON | Burlington | WI | 250 | 140.21 |
| NORTHWEST BK LACROSSE NA | La Crosse | WI | 247 | 234.24 |
| FIRST NB OF KENOSHA | Kenosha | WI | 239 | 364.52 |
| FIRST WISCONSIN BK MAYFAIR | Wauwatosa | WI | 238 | 109.23 |
| KELLOGG CITIZENS NB | Green Bay | WI | 238 | 636.59 |
| FIRST WISCONSIN NB | Madison | WI | 234 | 639.35 |
| FIRST WISCONSIN NB | Sheboygan | WI | 232 | 399.35 |
| FIRST WISCONSIN NB | Oshkosh | WI | 231 | 222.54 |
| BANK ONE WEST BEND | West Bend | WI | 230 | 129.13 |
| BANK ONE STEVENS POINT NA | Stevens Point | WI | 230 | 141.23 |
| BANK ONE BEAVER DAM | Beaver Dam | WI | 228 | 139.60 |
| ASSOCIATED BK LAKESHORE NA | Manitowoc | WI | 226 | 233.47 |
| M&I FIRST NB | West Bend | WI | 226 | 179.80 |
| FIRST WISCONSIN BK | Green Bay | WI | 218 | 149.88 |

# Top Rated U.S. Banks

|  |  |  | | |
|---|---|---|---|---|
| WAUKESHA ST BK | Waukesha | WI | 217 | 267.17 |
| FIRST NB OF CHIPPEWA | Chippewa Falls | WI | 217 | 121.47 |
| BANK ONE MADISON | Madison | WI | 217 | 267.63 |
| PARK BK | Milwaukee | WI | 215 | 203.90 |
| FIRST BANKING CENTER—BURLINGTON | Burlington | WI | 215 | 124.31 |
| FIRST WISCONSIN NB | Eau Claire | WI | 214 | 238.31 |
| FIRST WISCONSIN BK | Racine | WI | 214 | 119.65 |
| FIRST WISCONSIN NB | Milwaukee | WI | 213 | 3,435.25 |
| NATIONAL BK OF CMRC IN SUPERIOR | Superior | WI | 212 | 143.18 |
| M&I COMMUNITY STATE BK | Eau Claire | WI | 211 | 106.36 |
| BANK OF STURGEON BAY | Sturgeon Bay | WI | 209 | 177.19 |
| FIRST WISCONSIN NB | Manitowoc | WI | 208 | 125.79 |
| NORTHWESTERN BK | Chippewa Falls | WI | 204 | 109.06 |
| CENTRAL B&TC | Marshfield | WI | 204 | 100.81 |
| BANK ONE GREEN BAY | Green Bay | WI | 202 | 419.58 |
| FIRST NB OF RIVER FALLS | River Falls | WI | 202 | 101.46 |
| VALLEY BK | Appleton | WI | 200 | 536.93 |
| JACKSON ST BK | Jackson | WY | 234 | 143.25 |
| ROCK SPRINGS NB | Rock Springs | WY | 212 | 189.92 |
| KEY BK WYOMING | Riverton | WY | 209 | 167.67 |
| BANK OF GUAM | Agana | GU | 235 | 468.68 |
| SCOTIABANK DE PUERTO RICO | San Juan | PR | 226 | 583.67 |

*Concluded*

# Like A Bulging Wall

| Name | City | State | IDC Rank | Assets (Mill. $) |
|---|---|---|---|---|
| FIRST FEDERAL SAVINGS BANK | Decatur | AL | 235 | 227.16 |
| FIRST AMERICAN FS&LA | Huntsville | AL | 206 | 457.51 |
| FIRST FS&LA | Texarkana | AR | 211 | 119.60 |
| BEVERLY HILLS FEDERAL SVG BK | Beverly Hills | CA | 300 | 1,464.73 |
| STANDARD SAVINGS BANK | Los Angeles | CA | 300 | 236.23 |
| STERLING S&LA | Irvine | CA | 300 | 146.04 |
| WATSONVILLE FS&LA | Watsonville | CA | 300 | 135.35 |
| FIRST PUBLIC SAVINGS BANK | Los Angeles | CA | 286 | 194.51 |
| LUTHER BURBANK S&LA | Santa Rosa | CA | 271 | 222.01 |
| NEW HORIZONS S&LA | San Rafael | CA | 268 | 233.23 |
| ENCINO SAVINGS BANK | Encino | CA | 263 | 191.22 |
| HAWTHORNE S&LA | Hawthorne | CA | 258 | 1,057.99 |
| SACRAMENTO SAVINGS BANK | Sacramento | CA | 254 | 2,370.74 |
| INLAND S&LA | Hemet | CA | 251 | 111.15 |
| CITIBANK, F.S.B. | San Francisco | CA | 248 | 7,009.54 |
| TORRANCE S&LA | Torrance | CA | 242 | 121.65 |
| FIRST FEDERAL BK OF CALIFORNIA, FS | Santa Monica | CA | 241 | 2,826.58 |
| NORTHBAY SAVINGS BANK | Petaluma | CA | 239 | 240.22 |
| QUAKER CITY FS&LA | Whittier | CA | 238 | 353.65 |
| AMERICAN SAVINGS BANK, FA | Stockton | CA | 223 | 16,448.10 |
| POMONA FIRST FS&LA | Pomona | CA | 220 | 1,342.08 |

176

|  |  |  | | |
|---|---|---|---|---|
| DOWNEY S&LA | Costa Mesa | CA | 217 | 4,027.16 |
| MUTUAL S&LA | Pasadena | CA | 214 | 372.25 |
| LA JOLLA SAVINGS BANK | La Jolla | CA | 212 | 146.28 |
| TOPA SAVINGS BANK | Los Angeles | CA | 212 | 550.88 |
| WORLD S&LA, A FS&LA | Oakland | CA | 211 | 20,749.46 |
| CALIFORNIA S&LA, A FEDERAL ASSN. | San Francisco | CA | 210 | 457.98 |
| HEART FS&LA | Auburn | CA | 206 | 900.83 |
| ITT FEDERAL BANK FSB | Newport Beach | CA | 206 | 1,110.06 |
| EUREKABANK, A FSB | San Carlos | CA | 203 | 1,749.71 |
| BEACH SAVINGS BANK | Huntington Beach | CA | 201 | 101.94 |
| COLUMBIA SAVINGS, A FS&LA | Englewood | CO | 219 | 5,209.02 |
| BRISTOL FEDERAL SAVINGS BANK | Bristol | CT | 261 | 212.96 |
| FIRST FS&LA | Torrington | CT | 235 | 262.06 |
| FIRST FS&LA | East Hartford | CT | 208 | 425.27 |
| FIRST FS&LA | Waterbury | CT | 203 | 699.73 |
| GREENWICH FS&LA | Greenwich | CT | 201 | 261.20 |
| CITIBANK, FEDERAL SAVINGS BANK | Washington | DC | 293 | 1,191.30 |
| FIRST FSB OF CHARLOTTE COUNTY | Punta Gorda | FL | 277 | 348.55 |
| FIRST HOME FS&LA | Sebring | FL | 232 | 208.39 |
| CITIBANK, FEDERAL SAVINGS BANK | Miami | FL | 201 | 2,673.02 |
| THOMAS COUNTY, FS&LA | Thomasville | GA | 250 | 117.35 |

*Continued*

| Name | City | State | IDC Rank | Assets (Mill. $) |
|------|------|-------|----------|------------------|
| GWINNETT FS&LA | Lawrenceville | GA | 248 | 266.27 |
| FIDELITY FEDERAL SAVINGS BANK | Dalton | GA | 237 | 208.71 |
| FIRST FSB OF BRUNSWICK GEORGIA | Brunswick | GA | 207 | 224.60 |
| FIRST FS&LA OF AMERICA | Honolulu | HI | 269 | 800.07 |
| PIONEER FEDERAL SAVINGS BANK | Honolulu | HI | 211 | 572.79 |
| SECURITY FS&LA OF CHICAGO | Chicago | IL | 295 | 197.42 |
| CITIBANK, FEDERAL SAVINGS BANK | Chicago | IL | 270 | 5,005.60 |
| LIBERTY BANK FOR SAVINGS | Chicago | IL | 269 | 464.24 |
| NORTH SHORE S&LA | Waukegan | IL | 265 | 164.61 |
| DEERFIELD FS&LA | Deerfield | IL | 262 | 261.16 |
| EUREKA S&LA OF LA SALLE | La Salle | IL | 259 | 202.97 |
| ELMHURST FEDERAL SAVINGS BANK | Elmhurst | IL | 258 | 341.04 |
| SECOND FS&LA OF CHICAGO | Chicago | IL | 253 | 147.80 |
| HOYNE S&LA | Chicago | IL | 251 | 284.23 |
| PATHWAY FINANCIAL, A FEDERAL ASSN | Chicago | IL | 246 | 1,084.85 |
| FIRST FS&LA OF DES PLAINES | Des Plaines | IL | 245 | 318.92 |
| REGENCY SAVINGS BANK, A FSB | Naperville | IL | 241 | 320.96 |
| FIRST FSB OF PROVISO TOWNSHIP | Hillside | IL | 239 | 231.44 |
| OLNEY S&LA | Olney | IL | 232 | 155.22 |
| FIRST FS&LA OF WESTCHESTER | Westchester | IL | 228 | 236.93 |
| BELL FS&LA | Chicago | IL | 226 | 1,811.27 |

# Top Rated Savings and Loans

|  |  |  | | |
|------|------|-------|---|---|
| SOUTHWEST FS&LA OF CHICAGO | Chicago | IL | 224 | 252.95 |
| LIBERTY FS&LA OF CHICAGO | Chicago | IL | 224 | 408.97 |
| NORTHWESTERN S&LA | Chicago | IL | 219 | 1,370.84 |
| GAGE PARK S&LA | Chicago | IL | 218 | 115.16 |
| HOMEBANC, A FEDERAL SAVINGS BANK | Rockford | IL | 217 | 353.16 |
| ELGIN FEDERAL FIN CENTER, A FIN ASSN | Elgin | IL | 216 | 219.75 |
| CALUMET FS&LA | Chicago | IL | 212 | 398.29 |
| STERLING FEDERAL BANK, F.S.B. | Sterling | IL | 207 | 155.17 |
| FIRST FED SAVINGS BK OF MARION | Decatur | IL | 206 | 245.27 |
| FIRST FED SAVINGS BK OF KOKOMO | Champaign | IL | 205 | 116.02 |
| COMMUNITY SAVINGS BANK | Chicago | IL | 200 | 245.21 |
| PEOPLES FSB OF DEKALB COUNTY | Auburn | IN | 298 | 185.63 |
| WORKINGMENS FS&LA | Bloomington | IN | 280 | 147.22 |
| LINCOLN FEDERAL SAVINGS BANK | Plainfield | IN | 279 | 134.38 |
| AMERICANA SAVINGS BANK, FSB | New Castle | IN | 266 | 275.32 |
| FIRST FED SAVINGS BK OF MARIO | Marion | IN | 254 | 162.13 |
| FIRST FED SAVINGS BK OF KOKO | Kokomo | IN | 242 | 157.11 |
| MISHAWAKA FEDERAL SAVINGS | Mishawaka | IN | 240 | 149.21 |
| REGIONAL FEDERAL SAVINGS BANK | New Albany | IN | 236 | 152.42 |
| PEOPLES BANK, A FSB | Munster | IN | 234 | 209.18 |
| FIRST FS&LA OF RICHMOND | Richmond | IN | 219 | 155.47 |
| GREAT LAKES BANCORP IN, A FSB | Indianapolis | IN | 217 | 151.26 |
| FIRST FEDERAL SAVINGS BANK | Evansville | IN | 217 | 108.67 |
| INDIANA FS&LA | Valparaiso | IN | 214 | 542.90 |

*Continued*

| Name | City | State | IDC Rank | Assets (Mill. $) |
|---|---|---|---|---|
| PEOPLES FEDERAL SAVINGS ASSN | Richmond | IN | 212 | 153.70 |
| HOME LOAN SAVINGS BANK | Fort Wayne | IN | 210 | 168.08 |
| FIRST FS&LA OF LINCOLN—IOWA | Council Bluffs | IA | 286 | 136.69 |
| FIRST FSB OF FORT DODGE | Fort Dodge | IA | 202 | 134.57 |
| CAPITOL FS&LA | Topeka | KS | 251 | 3,278.37 |
| INTER-STATE FS&LA OF KANSAS CITY | Kansas City | KS | 233 | 237.50 |
| FIRST FSB OF ELIZABETHTOWN | Elizabethtown | KY | 300 | 199.72 |
| LEXINGTON FEDERAL SAVINGS BANK | Lexington | KY | 280 | 174.77 |
| FIRST FS&LA | Bowling Green | KY | 254 | 236.81 |
| GREAT FINANCIAL FEDERAL | Louisville | KY | 227 | 1,085.90 |
| FIRST FS&LA | Lexington | KY | 209 | 133.00 |
| GARDINER SAVINGS INSTITUTION, FSB | Gardiner | ME | 251 | 145.85 |
| MID MAINE SAVINGS BANK F.S.B | Auburn | ME | 209 | 147.99 |
| CUSTOM SAVINGS BANK, FSB | Baltimore | MD | 288 | 276.78 |
| REISTERSTOWN FEDERAL SAVINGS BANK | Reisterstown | MD | 266 | 215.98 |
| LAUREL FEDERAL SAVINGS BANK | Laurel | MD | 261 | 101.72 |
| ROSEDALE FS&LA | Baltimore | MD | 259 | 260.90 |
| ST. CASIMIRS S&LA | Baltimore | MD | 235 | 100.18 |
| HAMILTON FS&LA | Baltimore | MD | 227 | 116.68 |

180

## Top Rated Savings and Loans

|  |  |  | | |
|---|---|---|---|---|
| LEEDS FS&LA | Baltimore | MD | 223 | 189.61 |
| KEY FEDERAL SAVINGS BANK | Randallstown | MD | 218 | 186.18 |
| CHEVY CHASE SAVINGS BANK, FSB | Chevy Chase | MD | 214 | 5,174.39 |
| HARBOR FS&LA | Baltimore | MD | 212 | 115.74 |
| ARUNDEL FS&LA | Baltimore | MD | 206 | 157.31 |
| FIRST FSB OF WESTERN MARYLAND | Cumberland | MD | 201 | 338.26 |
| MIDDLESEX FS&LA | Somerville | MA | 260 | 108.47 |
| STERLING SAVINGS BANK, FSB | Southfield | MI | 300 | 144.06 |
| FIRST SECURITY SAVINGS BANK, FSB | Bloomfield Hills | MI | 299 | 102.51 |
| FIRST FS&LA OF LENAWEE COUNTY | Adrian | MI | 297 | 221.53 |
| WOLVERINE FS&LA | Midland | MI | 219 | 106.16 |
| DEARBORN FSB | Dearborn | MI | 217 | 202.94 |
| LASALLE FEDERAL SAVINGS BANK | Buchanan | MI | 215 | 100.07 |
| OTTAWA SAVINGS BANK FSB | Holland | MI | 202 | 240.61 |
| COMMUNITY FS&LA | Tupelo | MS | 257 | 115.39 |
| MACON B&LA | Macon | MO | 284 | 103.72 |
| THE CAMERON S&LA | Cameron | MO | 235 | 123.34 |
| KIRKSVILLE S&LA | Kirksville | MO | 209 | 108.26 |
| GREAT SOUTHERN S&LA | Springfield | MO | 206 | 468.37 |
| UNITED S&LA | Lebanon | MO | 200 | 437.51 |
| FIRST FEDERAL SAVINGS BANK OF MONTANA | Kalispell | MT | 262 | 172.48 |

*Continued*

| Name | City | State | IDC Rank | Assets (Mill. $) |
|------|------|-------|----------|------------------|
| SALEM CO-OP BK | Salem | NH | 243 | 126.60 |
| FIRST S&LA OF NEW HAMPSHIRE | Exeter | NH | 242 | 156.67 |
| MILFORD CO-OP BK | Milford | NH | 228 | 103.86 |
| KEARNY FS&LA | Kearny | NJ | 294 | 555.44 |
| CHARTER FEDERAL SAVINGS BANK | Randolph Township | NJ | 283 | 288.29 |
| CENTURY FS&LA OF BRIDGETON | Bridgeton | NJ | 273 | 148.99 |
| MANASQUAN S&LA | Wall Township | NJ | 267 | 128.90 |
| MAYFLOWER SAVINGS BANK SLA | Livingston | NJ | 263 | 126.45 |
| BOILING SPRINGS S&LA | Rutherford | NJ | 239 | 400.36 |
| PULAWSKI SAVINGS BANK, SLA | South River | NJ | 234 | 313.53 |
| LAKEVIEW S&LA | Paterson | NJ | 232 | 197.96 |
| PAMRAPO SAVINGS BANK, SLA | Bayonne | NJ | 218 | 376.02 |
| STURDY S&LA | Stone Harbor | NJ | 215 | 185.04 |
| CLIFTON SAVINGS BANK SLA | Clifton | NJ | 212 | 243.37 |
| GSL SAVINGS BANK, SLA | Guttenberg | NJ | 212 | 117.16 |
| OCEAN FEDERAL SAVINGS BANK | Brick Town | NJ | 210 | 647.64 |
| LAKELAND SAVINGS BANK, SLA | Succasunna | NJ | 208 | 315.38 |
| NVE S&LA | Englewood | NJ | 207 | 308.10 |
| SOMERSET SAVINGS BANK, SLA | Bound Brook | NJ | 206 | 327.03 |
| FIRST HOME SAVINGS BANK, SLA | Penns Grove | NJ | 205 | 150.39 |
| CAPE SAVINGS BANK, SLA | Cape May Ct Hse | NJ | 201 | 190.16 |

182

# Top Rated Savings and Loans

|  |  |  | | |
|---|---|---|---|---|
| FIRST FEDERAL SAVINGS BANK | Roswell | NM | 216 | 135.75 |
| ALAMOGORDO FS&&LA | Alamogordo | NM | 213 | 106.70 |
| FIRST FS&LA OF MIDDLETOWN | Middletown | NY | 300 | 165.18 |
| THE LONG ISLAND CITY S&LA | Long Island City | NY | 290 | 335.36 |
| JAMAICA SAVINGS BANK FSB | Lynbrook | NY | 274 | 1,698.56 |
| MASPETH FS&LA | Maspeth | NY | 272 | 577.94 |
| EASTMAN S&LA | Rochester | NY | 251 | 750.75 |
| RELIANCE FEDERAL SAVINGS BANK | Garden City | NY | 242 | 710.09 |
| THE LONG ISLAND SAVINGS BK, FSB | Syosset | NY | 219 | 2,675.11 |
| ASTORIA FS&LA | Long Island City | NY | 214 | 3,080.54 |
| SOUND FS&LA | Mamaroneck | NY | 209 | 145.90 |
| GEDDES FS&LA | Syracuse | NY | 207 | 125.46 |
| BROOKLYN FEDERAL SAVINGS BANK | Brooklyn | NY | 201 | 153.32 |
| WORKMENS FEDERAL SAVINGS BANK | Mount Airy | NC | 300 | 247.74 |
| CITIZENS S&LA | Lenoir | NC | 288 | 117.50 |
| PIEDMONT FS&LA | Winston-Salem | NC | 286 | 495.05 |
| HOME FEDERAL SAVINGS BANK | Salisbury | NC | 280 | 220.63 |
| MUTUAL FS&LA, A STOCK CORP. | Elkin | NC | 272 | 133.26 |
| HOME S&LA | Durham | NC | 270 | 239.71 |
| HAYWOOD S&LA | Waynesville | NC | 269 | 126.27 |
| GRAHAM S&LA | Graham | NC | 265 | 102.68 |
| COMMUNITY FS&LA | Burlington | NC | 262 | 130.48 |
| FIRST FSB OF MOORE COUNTY | Southern Pines | NC | 258 | 189.85 |

*Continued*

| Name | State | City | IDC Rank | Assets (Mill. $) |
|---|---|---|---|---|
| FIRST FEDERAL SAVINGS BANK | NC | Winston-Salem | 244 | 356.17 |
| HOME FS&LA | NC | Fayetteville | 240 | 155.84 |
| SECURITY FEDERAL SAVINGS BANK | NC | Durham | 232 | 261.58 |
| FIRST FS&LA OF PITT COUNTY | NC | Greenville | 225 | 138.32 |
| HOME FS&LA | NC | Charlotte | 223 | 552.88 |
| SECURITY S&LA | NC | Southport | 215 | 115.60 |
| PEOPLES FS&LA | NC | Thomasville | 213 | 104.01 |
| MUTUAL S&LA | NC | Lenoir | 209 | 102.33 |
| OLD STONE BANK OF N CAROLINA, A FSB | NC | High Point | 205 | 581.15 |
| HOME FS&LA | NC | Kings Mountain | 204 | 102.70 |
| GATE CITY FS&LA | NC | Greensboro | 203 | 464.74 |
| WORLD S&LA OF OHIO | OH | Stubenville | 300 | 411.10 |
| FALLS SAVINGS BANK, FSB | OH | Cuyahoga Falls | 277 | 305.43 |
| PERPETUAL FS&LA | OH | Urbana | 263 | 122.50 |
| SPRINGFIELD FS&LA | OH | Springfield | 251 | 118.80 |
| FIRST FS&LA | OH | Youngstown | 247 | 412.80 |
| THIRD FS&LA | OH | Cleveland | 239 | 2,807.26 |
| FIRST FINANCIAL SA, FA | OH | Cincinnati | 232 | 179.44 |
| INDUSTRIAL S&LA | OH | Bellevue | 226 | 196.76 |
| THIRD S&L CO | OH | Piqua | 225 | 119.75 |
| FIRST FS&LA | OH | Defiance | 222 | 373.38 |

184

# Top Rated Savings and Loans

| | | | | |
|---|---|---|---|---|
| FIRST FS&LA | Lakewood | OH | 217 | 359.36 |
| COTTAGE SA,FA | Madeira | OH | 213 | 190.44 |
| STATE SAVINGS BANK | Columbus | OH | 211 | 1,438.71 |
| MECHANICS B&LC | Mansfield | OH | 211 | 166.90 |
| THRIFT S&LCO | Norwood | OH | 211 | 126.98 |
| FIDELITY FS&LA | Norwood | OH | 208 | 166.67 |
| FIRST FS&LA | Lorain | OH | 208 | 171.87 |
| CHEVIOT B&L CO | Cheviot | OH | 207 | 125.58 |
| FIRST FS&LA | Wooster | OH | 206 | 321.64 |
| MERIT SA | Cincinnati | OH | 206 | 109.78 |
| OAK HILLS S&L CO, FA | Cincinnati | OH | 202 | 136.65 |
| ENTERPRISE FS&LA | Lockland | OH | 200 | 118.00 |
| KLAMATH FIRST FS&LA | Klamath Falls | OR | 235 | 297.41 |
| HATBORO FS&LA | Hatboro | PA | 292 | 147.92 |
| SELLERSVILLE S&LA | Perkasie | PA | 276 | 131.00 |
| UNITED FEDERAL SAVINGS BANK | State College | PA | 275 | 487.07 |
| PRIME SAVINGS BANK FSB | Philadelphia | PA | 271 | 317.36 |
| ELLWOOD FSB | Ellwood City | PA | 268 | 212.46 |
| FIRST FINANCIAL SAVINGS ASSN | Downingtown | PA | 263 | 150.32 |
| ECONOMY SA | Aliquippa | PA | 260 | 130.71 |
| FRANKLIN FIRST FEDERAL SAVINGS BANK | Wilkes-Barre | PA | 256 | 846.76 |
| CHARLEROI FS&LA | Charleroi | PA | 235 | 167.42 |
| SEWICKLEY S&LA | Sewickley | PA | 234 | 135.32 |

*Continued*

185

| Name | City | State | IDC Rank | Assets (Mill. $) |
|------|------|-------|----------|------------------|
| FIRST FS&LA OF GREENE COUNTY | Waynesburg | PA | 231 | 298.98 |
| THIRD FS&LA OF PHILADELPHIA | Kulpsville | PA | 231 | 192.04 |
| RELIABLE S&LA | Bridgeville | PA | 226 | 124.87 |
| FIDELITY SA | Pittsburgh | PA | 217 | 163.07 |
| WILLOW GROVE FS&LA | Maple Glen | PA | 213 | 177.93 |
| PHOENIXVILLE FS&LA | Phoenixville | PA | 210 | 136.38 |
| CENTRAL PENNSYLVANIA SA | Shamokin | PA | 208 | 477.29 |
| WASHINGTON FSB | Washington | PA | 207 | 295.67 |
| HARLEYSVILLE SA | Harleysville | PA | 204 | 144.17 |
| YARDLEY BANK FOR SAVINGS, FSB | Yardley | PA | 203 | 116.41 |
| RELIANCE SA | Altoona | PA | 203 | 130.72 |
| FIRST FS&LA | Perkasie | PA | 203 | 264.61 |
| ELMWOOD FEDERAL SAVINGS BANK | Media | PA | 202 | 234.62 |
| OMNI SAVINGS BANK, FSB | Columbia | SC | 277 | 104.49 |
| UNITED SAVINGS BANK INC | Greenwood | SC | 274 | 277.35 |
| FIRST FS&LA | Spartanburg | SC | 221 | 250.56 |
| OCONEE S&LA | Seneca | SC | 204 | 184.55 |
| HOME FEDERAL SAVINGS BANK | Charleston | SC | 204 | 163.77 |
| HOME FS&LA OF UPPER EAST TENNESSEE | Johnson City | TN | 273 | 760.49 |
| ELIZABETHTON FS&LA | Elizabethton | TN | 272 | 139.84 |
| FIDELITY FEDERAL BANK, A FSB | Nashville | TN | 222 | 1,017.33 |
| HOME FEDERAL BANK OF TENNESSEE, FS | Knoxville | TN | 202 | 883.32 |

# Top Rated Savings and Loans

| Institution | City | State | | Assets |
|---|---|---|---|---|
| USAA FEDERAL SAVINGS BANK | San Antonio | TX | 30 | 962.40 |
| HEIGHTS OF TEXAS, FSB | Houston | TX | 288 | 1,398.87 |
| SAN ANTONIO FEDERAL SAVINGS BANK | Weslaco | TX | 236 | 311.26 |
| AMERICAN FEDERAL BANK FSB | Dallas | TX | 231 | 2,642.76 |
| FIRST GIBRALTAR BANK, FSB | Houston | TX | 223 | 9,034.63 |
| PACIFIC SOUTHWEST BANK, FSB | Corpus Christi | TX | 210 | 1,042.99 |
| UNITED SAVINGS BANK | Ogden | UT | 222 | 290.68 |
| CROSSLAND SAVINGS, FSB | Salt Lake City | UT | 209 | 2,850.73 |
| FREDERICKSBURG S&LA | Fredericksburg | VA | 279 | 432.75 |
| PROVIDENCE S&LA, A FA | Vienna | VA | 260 | 412.04 |
| FRANKLIN FS&LA | Richmond | VA | 245 | 316.26 |
| COMMUNITY FEDERAL SAVINGS BANK | Staunton | VA | 241 | 120.40 |
| CO-OPERATIVE SAVINGS BANK, FSB | Lynchburg | VA | 211 | 187.17 |
| WASHINGTON FS&LA | Seattle | WA | 300 | 2,623.16 |
| CONTINENTAL SAVINGS BANK | Seattle | WA | 300 | 236.81 |
| PIONEER FEDERAL SAVINGS BANK | Lynnwood | WA | 276 | 724.01 |
| YAKIMA FS&LA | Yakima | WA | 249 | 491.48 |
| UNITED S&LA | Seattle | WA | 242 | 124.16 |
| ABERDEEN FS&LA | Aberdeen | WA | 224 | 141.56 |
| FIRST FS&LA | Renton | WA | 222 | 206.77 |
| RIVERVIEW SAVINGS BANK | Camas | WA | 212 | 114.43 |

*Continued*

| Name | City | State | IDC Rank | Assets (Mill. $) |
|------|------|-------|----------|------------------|
| OLYMPIA FS&LA | Olympia | WA | 210 | 162.95 |
| FIRST EMPIRE FS&LA | Charleston | WV | 283 | 179.01 |
| HANCOCK COUNTY FS&LA | Chester | WV | 207 | 148.86 |
| TIME FEDERAL SAVINGS BANK | Medford | WI | 273 | 136.66 |
| SECURITY BANK S.S.B. | Milwaukee | WI | 269 | 2,137.92 |
| SOUTH MILWAUKEE S&LA | South Milwaukee | WI | 258 | 150.91 |
| KENOSHA S&LA | Kenosha | WI | 253 | 383.97 |
| TWIN CITY S&LA | Neenah | WI | 238 | 164.27 |
| WAUWATOSA S&LA | Wauwatosa | WI | 233 | 381.73 |
| FIRST NORTHERN SAVINGS BANK, SA | Green Bay | WI | 225 | 299.47 |
| KINNICKINNIC FS&LA | Milwaukee | WI | 222 | 144.89 |
| CONTINENTAL SAVINGS BANK, SA | Milwaukee | WI | 222 | 131.03 |
| OSHKOSH S&LA | Oshkosh | WI | 219 | 167.49 |
| DE PERE FS&LA | De Pere | WI | 219 | 104.70 |
| MUTUAL SAVINGS BANK OF WISCONSIN, S | Milwaukee | WI | 218 | 1,156.03 |
| FIRST FINANCIAL—PORT SVG BK, S | Port Washington | WI | 217 | 105.52 |
| GREAT MIDWEST S&LA | Brookfield | WI | 214 | 317.48 |
| UNITED S&LA | Sheboygan | WI | 209 | 320.70 |

188

# Bibliography

INTRODUCTION
1. Malabre, Alfred Jr., *Beyond Our Means,* Random House, 1987, p. XII.
2. Ibid, p. XV.
3. Friedman, Benjamin, *Day of Reckoning,* Random House, 1988, p. 4.
4. Ibid, p. 5.

CHAPTER ONE
1. UPI article, (referring to Congressional testimony of February, 1985), March 19, 1985.

CHAPTER TWO
1. *Newsweek,* September 11, 1989.
2. Friedman, p. 5.
3. PR Newswire (Speech to Los Angeles Chamber of Commerce), November 19, 1985.

CHAPTER THREE
1. *New York Times,* October 15, 1990.
2. Batra, Ravi, *Surviving the Great Depression of 1990,* Bantam, 1988, p. 25.
3. *St. Paul Pioneer Press,* October 4, 1989.
4. Ibid.

CHAPTER FOUR
1. Paris, Alexander, *The Coming Credit Collapse,* HMR Publishing, 1984, p. 94.
2. Ibid.

CHAPTER FIVE
1. Friedman, p. 211.
2. Ibid, p. 12.
3. Ibid, p. 6.
4. Ibid, p. 12-13.
5. Ibid, p. 42.

## CHAPTER SIX

1. *St. Paul Pioneer Press,* April 7, 1990.
2. *Los Angeles Times,* June 24, 1990.
3. Malabre, p. 142.
4. *St. Paul Pioneer Press,* April 5, 1989.
5. *Barrons,* December, 1988.
6. Ibid.
7. Ibid.
8. *Malabre,* p. 141.
9. Browne, Harry, *The Economic Timebomb,* St. Martins, 1989, p. 51.

## CHAPTER SEVEN

1. Friedman, p. 101.
2. Paris, p. 134.
3. AP article, April 23, 1989.
4. *Minneapolis Tribune,* August 27, 1989.
5. Ibid.
6. *Wall Street Journal,* October 9, 1990.
7. Friedman, p. 106.

## CHAPTER EIGHT

1. *St. Paul Pioneer Press,* October 26, 1987.
2. *Wall Street Journal,* December 12, 1988.
3. Malabre, p. 158.
4. *Wall Street Journal,* November 25, 1988.

## CHAPTER NINE

1. *St. Paul Pioneer Press,* October 23, 1990.

## CHAPTER TEN

1. *St. Paul Pioneer Press,* October 11, 1990.
2. Ibid.
3. Paris, p. 15.

## CHAPTER ELEVEN

1. Gothard, Bill, *Mens' Manual Volume II,* Institute in Basic Youth Conflicts, 1983, p. 78-81.

# Bibliography

## OTHER SOURCES

Malabre, Alfred Jr., *Beyond Our Means*, New York, New York: Random House, 1987.

Friedman, Benjamin, *Day of Reckoning*, New York, New York: Random House, 1988.

Paris, Alexander, *The Coming Credit Collapse*, Barrington, Illinois: HMR Publishing, 1984.

Browne, Harry, *The Economic Time Bomb*, 175 5th Avenue, New York, New York: St. Martin's Press, 1989.

Batra, Ravi, *How to Survive the Depression of 1990*, 666 5th Avenue, New York, New York: Bantam Doubleday—Dell Publishing Group Inc., 1988.

Gothard, Bill, *Men's Manual Volume II*, Institute in Basic Youth Conflicts, Box 1, Oak Brook, Illinois, 60521, 1983.

Periodicals used:

*St. Paul Pioneer Press*
*Barrons*
*Wall Street Journal*
*New York Times*
*Minneapolis Tribune*
*Newsweek*